J.D. PONCE ON PROPHET MUHAMMAD

AN ACADEMIC ANALYSIS OF THE QURAN

© 2024 by J.D. Ponce

INDEX

PRELIMINARY CONSIDERATIONS ---5

Chapter I: MUHAMMAD – THE PATH TO ILUMINATION-----------------------8

Chapter II: THE ARAB WORLD IN THE TIME OF THE PROPHET---------17

Chapter III: CORE THEOLOGICAL PRINCIPLES IN THE QURAN---------22

Chapter IV: THE ONENESS OF GOD---24

Chapter V: DEVOTION TO GOD ALONE---30

Chapter VI: PROPHETS AND ANGELS --38

Chapter VII: JUDGMENT DAY---45

Chapter VIII: ETERNAL LIFE ---55

Chapter IX: ETHICAL CONDUCT --65

Chapter X: CALLS TO WORSHIP AND WARNINGS OF JUDGMENT-----69

Chapter XI: SOCIAL RESPONSIBILITIES --------------------------------------75

Chapter XII: THE FASTING OF RAMADAN-------------------------------------79

Chapter XIII: PRAYERS AND GLORIFICATIONS -------------------------------90

Chapter XIV: THE PURPOSE OF LIFE---98

Chapter XV: WORLDLY PLEASURES---104

Chapter XVI: DIVINE VIGILANCE, RESTLESSNESS, AND THRONE---108

Chapter XVII: THE UNSHARED AUTHORITY OF THE CREATOR--------110

Chapter XVIII: COSMIC ORDER---114

Chapter XIX: SIGNS IN THE STARS--118

Chapter XX: THE CREATOR OF LIFE, DEATH, AND THE UNIVERSE--127

Chapter XXI: SATAN'S ROLE AND INFLUENCE ------------------------------137

Chapter XXII: THE LEGACY OF ADAM AND EVE----------------------------142

Chapter XXIII: PROPHETHOOD OF JESUS---151

Chapter XXIV: THE BROTHERHOOD OF HUMANITY----------------------160

Chapter XXV: THE ESSENCE OF FEARING GOD---------------------------168

Chapter XXVI: REPENTANCE---175

Chapter XXVII: ADULTERY AND IDOLATRY----------------------------------185

Chapter XXVIII: FAITH AS A WAY OF LIFE------------------------------------190

Chapter XXIX: DEATH--201

Chapter XXX: LIFE AFTER DEATH --209

Chapter XXXI: 50 KEY QUOTES FROM THE PROPHET MUHAMMAD-217

PRELIMINARY CONSIDERATIONS

The Quran, the holy book of Islam, holds a central position in the lives of over a billion people around the world. Written in classical Arabic, it is organized in 114 surahs and 6,348 verses (including the Basmala), or 6,236 (if the Basmala is excluded). It emerged in the Arabian Peninsula in the 7th century. Its revelation to the Prophet Muhammad over a span of twenty-three years (610–632 CE) played a pivotal role in shaping the early Muslim community and continues to influence the Islamic civilization today. The linguistic richness and eloquence of the Quranic text have been acclaimed by scholars and believers alike, with its verses revered for their literary beauty and meaning.

The compilation of the Quran began during the lifetime of the Prophet Muhammad. The revelations started in the Night of Power and lasted over two decades, first in the city of Mecca and then in Medina, and they all were given in the Arabic language. These revelations were memorized by the early followers of Islam and also recorded in writing on various materials such as parchment, stone, and leather. The primary method of preservation initially involved committing the verses to memory, given the high level of importance attached to oral transmission in pre-Islamic Arab society.

Following the death of the Prophet Muhammad, the caliphate of Abu Bakr took proactive steps to ensure the preservation of the Quranic text. Under the guidance of the companion Zaid ibn Thabit, a committee was formed to collect and compile all available written and oral records of the Quran into a single manuscript. This standardized compilation was meticulously cross-verified with the memories of the companions who had memorized the Quran under the direct supervision of the Prophet.

Subsequent to this initial compilation, the third caliph, Uthman ibn Affan, undertook further measures to enhance the preservation of the Quran. Recognizing variations in the recitation of the Quran due to regional dialects, he commissioned the production of multiple copies of the standardized text and distributed them to different regions within the Islamic empire. This dissemination ensured uniformity in the recitation and preservation of the Quran across diverse linguistic and cultural contexts.

The rigorous methods employed by early Muslim scholars demonstrate their unwavering commitment to ensuring the accuracy and authenticity of the Quranic text. This comprehensive effort has played a pivotal role in the preservation of the Quran in its original form, making it one of the few religious texts that has been transmitted with an unparalleled degree of precision and fidelity over the centuries.

At its core, the Quran serves as a guide, offering insights into the nature of existence, moral conduct, justice, and spirituality. It addresses the fundamental questions of human existence and provides a framework for personal and communal flourishing. The Quran's emphasis on compassion, justice, equality, and the sanctity of life continues to offer guidance in addressing pressing global concerns such as poverty, conflict, environmental degradation, and social inequality.

Moreover, the Quran's rich language and literary style have fascinated generations of linguists, poets, and scholars. It's structure and rhetorical devices continue to captivate the minds of academics, inspiring research and analysis across diverse fields such as linguistics, literature, and semiotics.
The Quran's perspectives on science, nature, and cosmology have spurred contemplation and exploration, sparking dialogue between faith and reason. It's invitations to observe the

natural world, reflect on the signs of creation, and seek knowledge have contributed to the development of scientific inquiry and environmental ethics, fostering a harmonious relationship between humanity and the natural world.

In an increasingly interconnected global community, the Quran continues to serve as a source of intercultural dialogue and understanding. Through its ethical and spiritual teachings, it promotes mutual respect, tolerance, and cooperation among diverse civilizations and cultures, thereby contributing to the advancement of a more harmonious and peaceful world.

Chapter I
MUHAMMAD – THE PATH TO ILUMINATION

Muhammad Ibn ʿAbd Allāh ibn ʿAbd al-Muṭṭalib ibn Hāshim ibn ʿAbd Manāf ibn Quṣayy ibn Kilāb, the Prophet of Islam, was born into the powerful Quraysh tribe in Mecca in the year 570 AD. His father, Abdullah, died before his birth, leaving him orphaned at a young age. This early loss shaped Muhammad's understanding of empathy and compassion, as he experienced the pain of abandonment and the struggle to find his place in the world. His mother, Amina, also passed away when he was only six years old, further deepening his sense of vulnerability and isolation.

Raised by his grandfather, Abdul-Muttalib, and later by his uncle, Abu Talib, Muhammad developed a strong sense of familial loyalty and community support. These formative years instilled in him the values of honor, integrity, and respect for others, which would become foundational principles of his teachings later in life.

As a young boy, Muhammad spent time herding sheep in the outskirts of Mecca, honing his skills of observation and contemplation. This solitary existence in the serene surroundings of nature provided him with an opportunity for introspection and spiritual development. It was during these moments of solitude that he began to question the prevailing customs and beliefs of the society around him, eventually leading him to seek a deeper connection with the divine.

The influence of his family, particularly his beloved grandfather, Abdul-Muttalib, who was known for his wisdom and fair judgment, had an impact on Muhammad's character and outlook. The nurturing environment of love and guidance within his family instilled in him a deep sense of empathy and justice, which would be central to his mission as a prophet.

During his adolescence and early adulthood, Muhammad experienced a period of significant personal growth and development that shaped the foundations of his character and beliefs. His formative years were marked by a keen sense of curiosity and an innate quest for knowledge, which propelled him to engage actively with the intellectual and spiritual discourses of his time.

As a young man, Muhammad frequently sought solitude in the nearby caves of Mount Hira, contemplating the spirituality and socio-economic disparities that plagued Meccan society. These moments of introspection and contemplation would later serve as crucial incubators for the transformative experiences that defined his prophetic mission.

Muhammad's involvement in trade and commerce provided him with practical insights into human interactions, economics, and tribal alliances. These experiences not only sharpened his acumen but also cultivated a deep understanding of the social fabric underpinning the Arabian Peninsula.

His interactions with individuals from diverse backgrounds allowed him to witness firsthand the disparities and injustices prevalent in Meccan society, spurring within him a sense of compassion and empathy for the marginalized and oppressed. This empathy would form the cornerstone of his teachings and the nascent social justice movement that he would later champion.

Throughout this period, Muhammad demonstrated an unwavering commitment to honesty, integrity, and moral uprightness, earning him the title of Al-Amin, or the trustworthy, among his peers and associates. These attributes laid the groundwork for his future role as a unifier and exemplary leader, commanding respect and admiration from people across various strata of society.

The marriage of Prophet Muhammad to Khadijah, a prominent and successful businesswoman in Mecca, marked a significant turning point in his personal and economic growth. At the age of 25, Muhammad entered into a marriage that not only brought him love and companionship but also had an impact on his financial stability and social standing.

Khadijah, known for her intelligence, grace, and wisdom, was an influential figure in Meccan society. As a widow and successful merchant, she entrusted Muhammad with leading her trade caravans, thus providing him with valuable experience in commerce and exposing him to business dealings. This partnership not only enhanced Muhammad's financial acumen but also allowed him to build a reputation as a trustworthy and capable businessman in the community.

Moreover, Khadijah's unwavering support and belief in Muhammad played a pivotal role in shaping his self-confidence and sense of purpose. Her encouragement during moments of doubt and her steadfast belief in his character empowered Muhammad to front on to the challenges of his growing responsibilities both at home and in his budding role as a messenger of God.

The union with Khadijah not only enriched Muhammad's personal life but also provided him with a stable foundation from which to embark upon his spiritual journey. Her unwavering faith in his prophetic mission served as a source of strength and comfort, nurturing his spiritual development and fortifying his resolve during times of adversity.

In essence, the marriage to Khadijah was a catalyst for Muhammad's personal and economic growth, setting the stage for the transformative events that would shape the course of history. Their partnership exemplified mutual respect, unwavering support, and shared values, serving as a symbol of love, trust, and collaboration.

In the year 610 CE, a pivotal event occurred in the life of the Prophet Muhammad that would forever alter the course of history. It was during the holy month of Ramadan, while seeking solitude and spiritual contemplation in the Cave of Hira on the outskirts of Mecca, that Muhammad received his first divine revelation. The experience was awe-inspiring and overwhelming, as the Archangel Gabriel appeared before him and delivered the initial verses of what would later become the foundation of the Islamic faith.

This encounter marked the inception of Muhammad's prophetic mission and set in motion a series of revelations that would form the basis of the Quran, the sacred scripture of Islam. The impact of this momentous occasion cannot be overstated, as it signaled the commencement of a new era in the religious and social fabric of Arabia.

The revelation bestowed upon Muhammad brought forth a message of monotheism, moral rectitude, social justice, and compassion for the marginalized. These fundamental principles would become the cornerstones of his teachings and the framework for the transformation of Arabian society. In the face of prevailing idolatry, tribal warfare, and socio-economic disparities, the divine revelation served as a beacon of guidance and enlightenment, directing the Prophet and his followers toward a path of righteousness and egalitarianism.

The process of revelation continued over the span of 23 years, during which time Muhammad received divine guidance on various aspects of faith, ethics, jurisprudence, and governance. Each revelation addressed the specific needs and challenges encountered by the nascent Muslim community, providing practical solutions and spiritual nourishment. The Quranic injunctions urged believers to uphold integrity, uphold the rights of others, and promote harmony within the community and beyond.

As the bearer of these divine revelations, Muhammad assumed the role of a messenger and exemplar, conveying the word of God with unwavering conviction and humility. His steadfast commitment to disseminating the divine message amidst adversities and opposition exemplified his resolute dedication to his prophetic mission. The revelations not only served as a source of spiritual guidance but also as a catalyst for societal reform, fostering a sense of unity and solidarity among the disparate tribes and social strata.

During the Meccan period of Muhammad's life, he faced numerous challenges and obstacles as he began to preach his message and teachings. This period marked the commencement of his prophetic mission and the dissemination of the fundamental principles of Islam. Despite the significance of his message, Muhammad encountered strong resistance from the Meccan society, particularly from the leaders and the influential figures who were deeply entrenched in the traditional polytheistic beliefs. The initial teachings focused on the oneness of God, social justice, moral principles, and the accountability of individual actions in the Hereafter.

Muhammad's unwavering commitment to these teachings led to opposition and persecution from the powerful clans of Mecca. His followers, mostly marginalized and vulnerable members of society, also faced relentless persecution and discrimination. The early Muslims endured physical and emotional hardships, often resulting in social ostracism, economic boycotts, and even physical abuse. Despite these adversities, Muhammad remained steadfast in conveying his message of peace, coexistence, and compassion.

The struggles during the Meccan period also served as a testing ground for the faith and resilience of the nascent Muslim community. These challenges compelled them to demonstrate patience, fortitude, and solidarity while upholding their newfound faith. The endurance displayed by the early Muslims in the face of adversity became a testament to their unwavering commitment to the principles espoused by Muhammad.

Despite the arduous circumstances, Muhammad persevered in his mission, undeterred by the hardships he and his followers faced. His unwavering belief in the divine guidance bestowed upon him propelled him to continue preaching his message of monotheism and ethical conduct. Amidst the trials and tribulations, the Meccan period laid the groundwork for the moral and ethical framework of Islam, emphasizing virtues such as mercy, compassion, and justice.

Facing escalating persecution from the Meccan elites and seeking a safer environment to propagate the message of Islam, Muhammad and his followers embarked on a journey that would significantly shape the future of the Islamic community. The migration, known as the Hijra, not only provided physical safety but also laid the foundation for the establishment of the first Muslim community in Medina.

The decision to migrate was not made lightly. It required careful planning and strategic considerations to ensure the safety and well-being of the early Muslim community. This migration represented a shift from a position of vulnerability to one of greater autonomy and opportunity. It signaled a new phase in the prophetic mission, presenting unique challenges and opportunities for the nascent Muslim ummah.

Upon arrival in Medina, Muhammad's leadership and statesmanship came to the fore as he negotiated treaties and established a framework for governance and community life. The Constitution of Medina, a groundbreaking document that outlined the rights and responsibilities of various communities within Medina, exemplified Muhammad's vision for a pluralistic society based on justice and mutual respect.

The migration to Medina also brought about significant social and economic changes for the Muslim community. The bonds of brotherhood formed between the Muhajirun (migrants) and Ansar (helpers) fostered a spirit of solidarity and cooperation that became integral to the fabric of the Medinan society. This period witnessed the blossoming of a vibrant community committed to upholding the principles of faith, compassion, and social justice.

Moreover, the migration to Medina led to the expansion of Muhammad's mission beyond mere religious preaching. It involved the practical implementation of Islamic principles in a socio-political context, providing a template for future Muslim societies. The experiences gained during this critical phase laid the groundwork for the development of a distinctive Islamic ethos and governing model.

In the aftermath of the migration to Medina, Muhammad faced the formidable task of establishing a cohesive community and governance structure. This period marked a crucial juncture in the evolution of the nascent Muslim community, as it transitioned from a persecuted minority in Mecca to a thriving and organized entity in Medina.

Muhammad demonstrated remarkable diplomatic acumen and leadership skills in integrating the diverse tribal factions within Medina. He initiated the groundbreaking Constitution of Medina, which laid the groundwork for the harmonious coexistence of Muslims, Jews, and non-Muslim Arabs, underpinned by principles of mutual respect, cooperation, and social welfare. This pioneering document exemplified Muhammad's vision of an inclusive and pluralistic society, setting a precedent for governance and communal relations.

Furthermore, Muhammad's strategic foresight and administrative prowess fostered economic prosperity and social cohesion within the burgeoning Medina community. He implemented equitable policies to address socio-economic disparities, established systems for mutual support and charitable acts, and instilled a sense of collective responsibility among the residents of Medina.

Under Muhammad's guidance, the community also witnessed the development of a robust judicial system, which dispensed justice impartially and upheld the rights of both Muslims and non-Muslims. His emphasis on the rule of law and equitable treatment engendered a climate of stability and fairness, laying the groundwork for a just and orderly society.

One of the pivotal aspects of Medina's statecraft was the establishment of a unified defense strategy against external threats and internal discord. Muhammad's adeptness in forging alliances and treaties with neighboring tribes and city-states ensured the security and well-being of the Medina community. His adept diplomacy and military expertise were instrumental in safeguarding the fledgling Muslim polity from hostile forces and consolidating its position as a formidable entity in the region. The battles of Badr, Uhud, and the trench highlight the strategic acumen and unwavering resolve of the Prophet and his companions. Plus, the landmark treaties of

Hudaybiyyah and Al-Hudaybiyyah, exemplify Muhammad's adeptness in forging diplomatic solutions amidst conflict.

Throughout his final years, Muhammad dedicated himself to nurturing the next generation of leaders and reinforcing the principles of social justice and compassion. He sought to ensure a smooth transition of leadership and governance after his passing, emphasizing the importance of unity and cooperation among his followers.

As part of his legacy, Muhammad left behind a body of teachings and practices that continue to guide millions of Muslims around the globe. His emphasis on ethical conduct, social responsibility, and continuous self-improvement has contributed to the moral and spiritual development of countless individuals and communities.

Chapter II
THE ARAB WORLD IN THE TIME OF THE PROPHET

The Historical Landscape Prior to the Advent of Islam:

The historical landscape of the Arabian Peninsula prior to the advent of Islam is a tapestry woven with tribal dynamics, regional conflicts, and diverse religious beliefs. It was a time marked by both flourishing trade routes and lingering animosities among various tribes. The Arabian Peninsula, situated at the crossroads of continents, served as a nexus for commercial activities, connecting the Mediterranean world with the Indian Ocean. The cities of Mecca and Medina were bustling trade centers, attracting merchants and travelers from far-reaching lands.

In this socio-political milieu, the concept of honor and loyalty was deeply entrenched within the tribal societies. The Arabian people adhered to a code of conduct based on principles of kinship and allegiance, wherein tribal affiliations held utmost significance. Feuds between tribes were not uncommon, often stemming from disputes over resources, territory, or avenging past wrongs. These intertribal conflicts contributed to a complex and precarious social environment.

Moreover, the religious landscape of pre-Islamic Arabia comprised a multitude of faiths, including polytheistic beliefs, Christianity, Judaism, and indigenous spiritual practices. The Kaaba in Mecca, a revered sanctuary housing numerous idols, was a focal point of religious pilgrimage and ritualistic ceremonies. The diverse religious framework underscored the tolerance and syncretism prevalent in the region, albeit punctuated by occasional tensions and power struggles.

Social Structures and Tribal Dynamics in Pre-Islamic Arabia:

The pre-Islamic Arabian Peninsula was characterized by a complex web of tribal affiliations, with each tribe holding its own distinct customs, traditions, and hierarchy. Social status and honor were deeply intertwined with tribal affiliation, and allegiance to one's tribe was a cornerstone of individual identity. This network of tribes often led to both alliances and conflicts, influencing everything from trade and resource distribution to systems of governance.

Within the tribal structure, leadership was typically determined by a combination of lineage, military prowess, and charisma. The elders, known as the wise council of the tribe, held significant influence in decision-making processes and conflict resolution. Conversely, the younger generation sought to establish their authority through acts of courage, generosity, and displaying prowess in warfare and poetry.

The concept of 'asabiya,' or group solidarity, was fundamental in pre-Islamic Arab society. Loyalty to one's tribe was paramount, and any transgression against the honor or rights of a tribe member could lead to retaliatory actions, perpetuating cycles of violence and feuds. The difficulties of tribal dynamics also extended to economic activities, where trade routes, oasis territories, and commercial transactions were often governed by tribal agreements and disputes.

Moreover, social stratification within tribes was evident, with warriors and skilled artisans occupying positions of prestige, while slaves and marginalized individuals faced systemic discrimination and exploitation. Gender roles were also delineated within this social framework, with men primarily engaging in public affairs and warfare, while women were entrusted with domestic responsibilities and the preservation of familial honor.

Political Landscape in the 7th Century:

In the turbulent landscape of 7th century Arabia, the Peninsula was characterized by disparate tribal factions, each vying for dominance and control over valuable resources and territories. The web of alliances and rivalries often led to complex and volatile power dynamics, with shifting allegiances and strategic maneuvering defining the geopolitical landscape. At the heart of these power struggles lay the city of Mecca, a crucial hub for trade and commerce, where influential merchant families wielded significant influence over the region's affairs. The power struggles in Mecca were compounded by the emergence of Islam, which posed a formidable challenge to the existing power structures. As the Prophet Muhammad gained followers and sought to establish a new order based on the principles of monotheism and social justice, it ignited tensions and resistance from those who held vested interests in preserving the status quo. The political landscape was further complicated by external forces, including the Byzantine and Sassanian empires, whose imperial ambitions and struggle for regional hegemony intersected with the internal power dynamics of the Arabian Peninsula. These external pressures added an additional layer of complexity to the already web of alliances and power struggles, creating a volatile and unpredictable environment. Within this context, the political machinations and strategic maneuvering of various factions and leaders shaped the trajectory of early Islamic history, influencing pivotal events such as the Treaty of Hudaybiyyah and the eventual conquest of Mecca.

Religious Beliefs and Pagan Practices Before Islam:

Central to the religious tapestry of pre-Islamic Arabia were the polytheistic beliefs in multiple deities, each associated with different aspects of nature and human experiences. These deities were often worshipped through sacred stones, trees, or idols, symbolizing fertility, protection, and other earthly concerns. The sacred Kaaba in Mecca, which served as a major center for pilgrimage and trade, housed numerous idols representing these deities, thus underscoring the prevalent polytheistic belief system.

Moreover, the bedouin nomads and settled communities practiced various rituals and ceremonies to appease their deities, seeking protection, good fortune, and blessings for their endeavors. Sacrificial offerings, divination practices, and communal gatherings formed integral parts of their religious customs, reflecting their deep-seated spiritual connection to the natural world and the unseen forces they believed governed their destinies.

Furthermore, alongside the polytheistic worship, animistic beliefs permeated the pre-Islamic Arabian spirituality. The natural elements, such as mountains, springs, and celestial bodies, were revered as manifestations of supernatural powers, embodying spirits and divine influences. This reverence for the natural environment underscored the mystical bond between the people of Arabia and the physical world around them, reinforcing the intertwined nature of their religious and cultural practices.

Asides from this, the concept of jinn, ethereal beings existing in a parallel realm, held an influential position in the pre-Islamic Arabian belief system. Stories about jinn encounters, magical phenomena, and other supernatural occurrences abounded, permeating the folklore and traditions of the people. The jinn were perceived as formidable entities with the ability to interfere in human affairs, serving as a source of both awe and apprehension among the inhabitants of ancient Arabia.

In addition to these religious beliefs, the institution of pilgrimage to the Kaaba and the practice of circumambulation (tawaf) around the sacred structure played a crucial role in the religious life of pre-Islamic Arabs, symbolizing unity, tradition, and communal identity. The annual pilgrimage drew people from all corners of the Arabian Peninsula, fostering commercial exchanges, social interactions, and the dissemination of cultural ideas, further enriching the interconnected tapestry of pre-Islamic Arabian society.

Intellectual Life and Cultural Exchanges in Early Arabia:

The intellectual life and cultural exchanges in early Arabia were dynamic and diverse, reflecting a society that was interconnected with neighboring civilizations and yet retained its distinctive identity. The Arabian Peninsula served as a crossroads for trade and cultural interactions, facilitating the exchange of ideas, beliefs, and practices among various communities. One of the most remarkable aspects of early Arabian intellectual life was its rich tradition of oral poetry. Poets held a revered status in society, as their eloquence and mastery of language were highly valued. They played a pivotal role in preserving and transmitting the history, customs, and moral values of their tribes through vibrant poetic compositions. These poets were not only entertainers but also historians, chroniclers, and philosophers, shaping the intellectual landscape of pre-Islamic Arabia. Moreover, the thriving trade networks in the region facilitated the exchange of knowledge and ideas with distant lands. The caravan routes that crisscrossed the desert brought merchants, travelers, and scholars from diverse backgrounds, leading to a blending of cultural influences. Arab merchants engaged in extensive trade with Byzantine and Sassanian territories, encountering and assimilating various philosophical, scientific, and artistic traditions. These interactions fostered an environment of cultural exchange and intellectual stimulation.

Chapter III
CORE THEOLOGICAL PRINCIPLES IN THE QURAN

The Quran, as the central religious text of Islam, expounds upon several core theological principles that underpin the faith and shape the worldview of Muslims. At the heart of these principles lies the concept of Tawhid, or the oneness of God. The Quran unequivocally asserts the monotheistic nature of God, emphasizing His absolute uniqueness and singularity. This foundational belief resonates throughout the Quran, serving as a constant reminder to devotees of the indivisible unity of the Divine.

Another vital theological principle enshrined in the Quran is the idea of divine justice and mercy. The Quranic verses often elucidate the balance between God's justice and compassion, portraying an equitable and benevolent Creator who oversees the affairs of humanity with fairness and magnanimity. The concept of divine justice incorporates notions of accountability, recompense, and the ultimate rectification of all injustices, while divine mercy offers solace and hope to believers amidst life's trials and tribulations.

Furthermore, the Quran articulates the significance of prophethood and revelation in conveying divine messages to humankind. It recognizes the pivotal role of prophets as intermediaries between God and humanity, charged with disseminating ethical guidance, moral injunctions, and warnings of impending consequences. Through narratives of earlier prophets and their communities, the Quran illustrates the perennial struggle between righteousness and iniquity, accentuating the relevance of ethical precepts across time and civilizations.

The concept of accountability before God infuses the Quran with a firm moral compass, underscoring the individual's autonomy and responsibility for their choices and actions. The Quran presents a comprehensive framework of moral and ethical standards, delineating the virtues of righteousness, patience, humility, and charity, whilst condemning vices such as injustice, arrogance, deceit, and oppression. By elucidating human conduct and emphasizing the virtue of sincere intention, the Quran engenders a conscientious awareness of one's moral agency and its implications in both worldly and spiritual domains.

In addition to these principles, the Quran expounds upon the nature of faith, resilience, and steadfastness in the face of adversity, providing solace and fortitude to believers during times of trial and testing. It stresses the impermanence of worldly life and underscores the transcendental nature of spiritual fulfillment, inspiring individuals to cultivate unwavering trust in God's wisdom and providence. The Quran thereby intertwines theological tenets with practical guidance, fostering a holistic approach to faith that encompasses belief, practice, and ethical comportment.

Chapter IV
THE ONENESS OF GOD

Tawhid - The Essence of Monotheism:

Tawhid, the central theological concept in Islam, embodies the belief in the oneness and unity of God. It serves as the foundation of Islamic faith, encapsulating the idea of divine singularity in its purest form. At its core, Tawhid represents the unique and exclusive nature of God's essence, attributes, and actions. This principle is deeply ingrained in the Quran, where the concept of Tawhid is repeatedly emphasized, affirming the indivisible nature of God. In Islamic theology, Tawhid pervades all aspects of belief, shaping the understanding of God's absolute unity and sovereignty over creation. The significance of Tawhid extends beyond mere acknowledgment of a singular deity; it encompasses the recognition of God as the ultimate source of guidance, power, and sustenance. Through Tawhid, Muslims are reminded of their responsibility to uphold and propagate the oneness of God, anchoring their spirituality in a devoted commitment to monotheism. Understanding Tawhid requires an exploration of its implications across various facets of human existence. From personal devotion to societal ethics, Tawhid permeates every dimension of a believer's life, fostering an unwavering connection to the divine. By comprehending the essence of Tawhid, individuals can gain a deeper insight into the inherent unity and coherence of creation, realizing the interconnectedness of all existence through the divine origin. Moreover, Tawhid engenders a spiritual equilibrium, offering solace and certainty in the face of life's adversities. It serves as a beacon, illuminating the path of believers and guiding them towards a harmonious relationship with God. Embracing Tawhid entails far more than a theoretical affirmation of monotheism; it necessitates an active, lived commitment to embodying the principles of divine unity in thoughts, words, and deeds. Thus, the overarching theme of Tawhid underscores the unparalleled significance of monotheism in Islamic spirituality, serving as a comprehensive framework that informs and shapes the worldview of Muslims across the globe.

Fundamental Beliefs:

Tawhid encapsulates the unequivocal monotheism that defines the Islamic faith. Central to this theological framework is the concept of the absolute unity of God, negating any notion of plurality or partners. It emphasizes the exclusive worship and devotion to the singular divine entity, devoid of any associations or intermediaries.

Fundamental beliefs in Tawhid encompass various dimensions, delving into the nature and attributes of God as expounded in the Quran and prophetic traditions. These beliefs center on affirming the absolute oneness of God in His lordship, divinity, and names and attributes. The understanding of Tawhid extends to acknowledging the uniqueness of God's sovereignty, the significance of His absolute authority over creation, and the affirmation of His incomparable attributes.

Moreover, the theological framework of Tawhid elucidates the concept of 'rububiyyah', which pertains to God's lordship and governance over the universe. This aspect underscores the omnipotence of God as the sustainer and provider, delineating the inherent oneness and mastery of His divine dominion. Concurrently, Tawhid al-uluhiyyah emphasizes the exclusive worship and adoration of God, rejecting all forms of idolatry or polytheism. It underscores the imperative of directing all acts of worship, veneration, and supplication solely to the divine entity, devoid of any rivals or associates.

Furthermore, the theological framework elucidates the concept of 'asma' wa-sifat', which pertains to the divine names and attributes. It encompasses an acknowledgment of the unique and unparalleled attributes of God, encapsulating His perfection, mercy, justice, and compassion. Embracing these fundamental beliefs in Tawhid engenders an understanding of the majestic and transcendent nature of God, fostering a deep sense of reverence and awe.

The Divine Singularity:

In delving into the concept of divine singularity, we are confronted with philosophical inquiries that seek to comprehend the nature of God's oneness. This fundamental aspect of Tawhid necessitates a comprehensive exploration into the philosophical underpinnings that underlie the unity of the Divine. Philosophical debates have arisen since antiquity, as scholars and theologians grapple with the nature of divine singular existence. Within this framework, philosophical examination revolves around the transcendence and immanence of God, and the reconciling of these seemingly opposing attributes within the context of Tawhid. Philosophers throughout history have sought to reconcile the absolute unity of God with the diversity and complexity observed in the world, contemplating the implications of divine singularity on the omnipotence and omniscience of the Creator. The question of how the infinite and incomprehensible nature of God's oneness interacts with the observable plurality of creation engenders rigorous intellectual discourse. Additionally, philosophical reflections on divine singularity extend to discussions on the divine attributes and their relationship to Tawhid, paving the way for nuanced examinations of divine essence, knowledge, and will. Through the lens of philosophical inquiry, one can illuminate the profundity of divine unity, offering insights into the interconnectedness of all existence and the unifying force of the divine essence.

Scriptural Evidence:

The concept of Tawhid, or the oneness of God, is emphatically underscored in various sacred texts across different religious traditions. In Islamic scripture, the Quran, the primary and most revered text, repeatedly emphasizes the absolute unity and indivisibility of Allah. Numerous passages unequivocally affirm that there is no deity except Allah, and encapsulate the essence of Tawhid. For instance, Surah Al-Ikhlas (Chapter 112) succinctly declares that Allah is One, Eternal, and Self-Sufficient, while Absolute Unity is echoed in Surah Al-An'am (Chapter 6) and Surah Maryam (Chapter 19). Similarly, in Christianity, central to the doctrine is the affirmation of monotheism, as reflected in passages from the Bible such as Deuteronomy 6:4 and Mark 12:29. These verses underscore the singular nature of God and reject the notion of associating partners with Him. Moreover, Jewish scripture, particularly the Shema Yisrael prayer found in the Torah (Deuteronomy 6:4–5), reiterates the belief in the oneness of God, imparting a testimony to divine unity. Hindu scriptures such as the Rigveda also uphold the principle of monotheism, exemplified in the hymn known as Purusha Sukta, which exalts the transcendental being as the primeval source of the universe. Additionally, echoes of divine singularity can be found in the Sikh scripture Guru Granth Sahib, emphasizing the uniqueness and omnipresence of the Supreme Being. The wealth of scriptural evidence from diverse religious traditions underscores the pervasive significance of Tawhid in shaping spiritual beliefs worldwide, serving as a testament to the universal appeal and relevance of monotheism.

Practical Implications - Living with Divine Oneness:

Living with the belief in divine oneness, or Tawhid, carries numerous practical implications that shape the daily lives of adherents. The understanding that there is no deity but God and that He is indivisible resonates deeply in every aspect of an individual's behavior, thoughts, and interactions with others. This belief serves as a guiding principle for fostering humility, gratitude, and a sense of accountability. Practically, the concept of Tawhid informs decision-making processes, ethical considerations, and personal conduct.

At its core, living with Tawhid entails cultivating a consciousness of God's presence in all facets of life. This awareness extends to acts of worship, such as prayer, fasting, and charity, as well as mundane activities like work, leisure, and social engagements. It prompts believers to uphold honesty, kindness, and justice in their relationships and dealings, recognizing that their conduct reflects their devotion to God's oneness. Moreover, Tawhid encourages individuals to seek excellence in their pursuits, to continuously strive for self-improvement, and to view challenges as opportunities for spiritual growth.

Additionally, embracing Tawhid influences the perspectives on material possessions and worldly ambitions. Adherents are encouraged to maintain detachment from material wealth, viewing it as a means to serve others rather than as an end in itself. The pursuit of wealth is balanced with the responsibility to contribute to the welfare of society, emphasizing the importance of charity and social welfare as integral components of faith. This perspective fosters a community ethos where individuals support one another, particularly in times of need, thereby embodying the values inherent in the belief in divine oneness.

Furthermore, the principle of Tawhid informs the mindset towards adversities and blessings in life. Adherents recognize that challenges serve as tests of faith and opportunities for spiritual endurance, resilience, and trust in divine wisdom. Conversely, moments of prosperity are viewed as blessings from God, calling for expressions of gratitude, generosity, and sharing with those less fortunate. This dynamic outlook enables individuals to find purpose and meaning in both trials and triumphs, anchoring them in a state of spiritual equilibrium.

Common Misinterpretations:

Misinterpretations and misconceptions regarding the concept of Tawhid have persisted throughout history, leading to a divergence from its true essence. One common misinterpretation is the conflation of Tawhid with mere monotheism. While monotheism acknowledges the existence of a single deity, Tawhid encompasses the oneness, uniqueness, and indivisibility of God in all aspects, including His lordship, names, attributes, and actions. This distinction is crucial in understanding the depth and significance of Tawhid. Another prevalent misconception is the reduction of Tawhid to a purely theoretical concept, detached from practical implications. In reality, Tawhid informs every facet of a believer's life, shaping their worldview, ethical conduct, and interpersonal relations. It serves as the foundation for an integrated and holistic approach to faith and living. Additionally, some may mistakenly perceive Tawhid as a rigid and exclusionary belief system, fostering an insular mindset. On the contrary, Tawhid emphasizes the universal message of divine unity, promoting inclusivity, compassion, and respect for all creation. It transcends barriers of race, ethnicity, and creed, uniting humanity under the banner of monotheism. Furthermore, misconceptions often arise from a superficial understanding of Tawhid, neglecting its theological depth and spiritual implications. As society grapples with diverse philosophical perspectives and ideological paradigms, clarifying these misconceptions is paramount in fostering interfaith dialogue, mutual understanding, and harmonious coexistence among religious communities.

Chapter V
DEVOTION TO GOD ALONE

Principles of Devotion in Islamic Faith:

In Islam, devotion to God is woven into the very fabric of life. The practice of worship, known as 'ibadah', extends beyond rituals and encompasses every action taken with a conscious intention to please God. This concept of devotion is rooted in the fundamental belief that God is the sole creator and sustainer of the universe, and all acts of worship are directed solely towards Him. Islamic faith emphasizes the unity, or 'tawhid', of God, rejecting any form of association or partnership with Him.

Central to the principles of devotion in Islamic faith is the concept of sincerity ('ikhlas') in all worshipping acts. Muslims are encouraged to perform their acts of worship purely for the sake of God, without seeking validation or approval from others. This principle instills humility, selflessness, and genuine piety in the worshipper, emphasizing the internal state of the heart and mind above outward displays of religiosity.

Furthermore, the five pillars of Islam – shahada (declaration of faith), salat (prayer), zakat (almsgiving), sawm (fasting), and hajj (pilgrimage) – serve as foundational practices that guide and perpetuate devotion in the lives of Muslims. These pillars form a framework for achieving spiritual purification, social welfare, and maintaining a steadfast connection with God through various forms of worship.

The Quran, considered the ultimate guide for Muslims, expounds on the principles of devotion by providing moral and spiritual guidance for adherents. It elucidates the significance of prayer, charity, fasting, and pilgrimage in nurturing a harmonious relationship with God and fostering a sense of community and justice among believers.

Moreover, the Prophet Muhammad's exemplary life serves as a model for understanding the principles of devotion in Islamic faith. His devotion to God and his unwavering commitment to spreading the message of monotheism inspire Muslims to emulate his conduct and teachings in their daily lives.

It is through upholding these principles that individuals in Islamic faith harness the transformative power of devotion, enriching their lives with a sense of purpose, connection to God, and responsibility towards fellow human beings. By adhering to these principles, Muslims strive to embody devotion in its truest form, seeking divine pleasure and striving for excellence in every aspect of their existence.

Unique Aspects of Islamic Monotheism:

Islamic monotheism, known as Tawhid, encompasses unique aspects that define its core belief system and distinguish it from other religious traditions. At the heart of Islamic monotheism is the concept of the absolute oneness and unity of Allah, the one and only God. This belief permeates every aspect of a Muslim's life and shapes their worldview, moral compass, and spiritual practices.

One of the distinctive features of Islamic monotheism is its uncompromising emphasis on the transcendence and absolute sovereignty of God. Muslims believe in the complete and unparalleled authority of Allah over the universe, affirming His omnipotence, omniscience, and omnipresence. This understanding fosters a sense of awe, reverence, and humility in the hearts of believers, encouraging them to submit to the divine will and seek closeness to God through sincere devotion.

Another noteworthy aspect of Islamic monotheism is the rejection of intermediaries between individuals and God. Unlike some belief systems, Islam advocates direct communication and connection with the Creator without the need for intercessors or mediators. This direct relationship underscores the personal responsibility of each individual to cultivate their faith, engage in righteous deeds, and seek divine guidance through prayer and supplication.

Furthermore, Islamic monotheism promotes a holistic integration of faith into all aspects of life, including social, ethical, and legal dimensions. The oneness of God serves as the foundation for establishing justice, compassion, and equity in human interactions and societal structures. By upholding the principles of Tawhid, Muslims strive to manifest the divine attributes of mercy, fairness, and generosity in their conduct, thereby nurturing harmonious relationships and fostering communal well-being.

Moreover, the monotheistic framework of Islam instills a deep sense of accountability and moral responsibility within individuals. The belief in the existence of a Day of Judgment and the reckoning of deeds reinforces the awareness that every action, intention, and thought is subject to divine scrutiny. This awareness motivates believers to uphold ethical standards, uphold integrity, and fulfill their obligations with diligence and sincerity.

Spiritual Practices and Their Significance:

In Islam, spiritual practices play a fundamental role in shaping the individual's connection with the divine and fostering a sense of inner peace and tranquility. These practices are not merely rituals confined to specific times or places; rather, they permeate every aspect of a believer's life, influencing their behavior, mindset, and character. The importance of spiritual practices lies in their ability to align individuals with the teachings of Islam, grounding them in a set of ethical values and principles that guide their interactions with themselves, others, and the world at large. Through these practices, Muslims aim to uphold their commitment to monotheism and cultivate a deep sense of gratitude, humility, and submission to the will of God.

Central to Islamic spiritual practices are the Five Pillars of Islam - Shahada (Declaration of Faith), Salat (Prayer), Zakat (Almsgiving), Sawm (Fasting during Ramadan), and Hajj (Pilgrimage to Mecca). Each pillar serves as a cornerstone of devotion and is deeply intertwined with the core tenets of monotheism. The rituals and acts associated with these pillars are not only outward expressions of faith but also serve as reminders of the believer's covenant with their Creator. By engaging in these practices, Muslims reaffirm their dedication to the oneness of God and embrace the responsibilities that spring from this belief.

Beyond the Five Pillars, other spiritual practices, such as dhikr (remembrance of God), dua (supplication), and seeking knowledge, carry great significance in nurturing an individual's spiritual well-being. Dhikr, the continuous remembrance of God through recitations and reflections, serves as a means of drawing closer to the divine presence and finding solace in moments of difficulty or joy. Similarly, dua, or personal supplication, allows believers to establish an intimate line of communication with Allah, seeking guidance, forgiveness, and blessings for themselves and others. Furthermore, the pursuit of knowledge, particularly religious education and spiritual enlightenment, is considered a commendable act in Islam, as it enables individuals to deepen their understanding of faith, morality, and the human experience.

The significance of these spiritual practices extends beyond individual fulfillment; they also foster a strong sense of communal unity and collective responsibility. When performed collectively, as seen in congregational prayers and communal acts of charity, these practices reinforce the bond among believers and emphasize the reciprocal obligations they hold towards one another. This communal aspect highlights the interconnectedness of individuals in their journey of faith, emphasizing the shared commitment to upholding the principles of monotheism and righteousness.

Centrality of Prayer in Devotional Life:

Prayer serves as a direct means of establishing a personal connection with the Divine and exemplifies the key tenets of monotheistic worship. Through regular prayer, a believer affirms the submission to God and acknowledges His omnipotence, mercy, and grace. It is a solemn act that fosters mindfulness and spiritual discipline, grounding individuals in remembrance and reverence.

The five daily prayers, known as Salat, are prescribed at specific times throughout the day, serving to structure and sanctify a Muslim's daily routine. This regular rhythm of prayer punctuates the passing hours, ensuring that the remembrance of God becomes an integral part of everyday life. This observance also reinforces the understanding that all aspects of life should be infused with spirituality and devotion.

Each prayer, from the pre-dawn Fajr to the night-time Isha, offers an opportunity for introspection, gratitude, and supplication. Engaging in ritual purification before each prayer underscores the importance of spiritual cleanliness and readiness for encountering the Divine presence. The physical postures of prayer, including standing, bowing, prostrating, and sitting, symbolize humility, surrender, and submission to the will of God. Through these actions, a worshipper embodies a state of spiritual and physical surrender, establishing a harmonious balance between the material and the spiritual realms.

Furthermore, congregational prayers held in mosques provide a communal dimension to this individual act of worship. They foster a sense of unity, mutual support, and collective devotion, strengthening the bonds of brotherhood and sisterhood within the community. Additionally, the Friday congregational prayer, known as Jumu'ah, serves as a gathering wherein believers receive religious exhortation, guidance, and encouragement, promoting social cohesion and a deeper understanding of faith.

The concept of prayer in Islam extends beyond the formal acts of worship to encompass the continuous remembrance of God throughout one's daily activities. This ongoing mindfulness allows for the maintenance of a perpetual connection to the Divine, infusing mundane tasks with purpose and spiritual meaning. Thus, prayer serves as a constant reminder of the transient nature of worldly pursuits and the eternal significance of the Hereafter.

The Role of the Quran in Worship:

The Quran holds an indispensable role in shaping the worship practices of Muslims. One of the fundamental aspects of the Quran's role in worship is its significance in ritual prayer. Recitation of verses from the Quran forms an integral part of the daily prayers performed by Muslims, serving as a direct means of communing with the Divine. The recitation of specific chapters and verses during different prayer cycles underscores the Quran's pivotal role in establishing a deep connection between the worshipper and the Creator.

Furthermore, the Quran provides a comprehensive framework for ethical behavior and righteous living, which permeates all facets of worship. Its teachings on compassion, justice, humility, and mercy inform the manner in which Muslims approach their acts of devotion, whether through formal prayers, charitable deeds, or personal supplications. This ethical dimension underscores the Quran's influence in shaping not only individual worship but also the broader communal practice of faith.

In addition to its immediate impact on worship rituals, the Quran also serves as a source of spiritual solace and guidance for Muslims in times of personal or collective challenges. Its wisdom offers a sense of reassurance and strength, inspiring believers to remain steadfast in their devotion and resilient in the face of adversity. The Quran's role in nurturing faith amidst trials and tribulations underscores its significance as a source of comfort and hope.

Moreover, the Quran's influence extends beyond the individual domain of worship, shaping the broader Islamic worldview and community identity. As a foundational text, it establishes the principles of monotheism, moral conduct, and social responsibility, guiding Muslims in their pursuit of a virtuous and God-conscious life. This holistic influence of the Quran underscores its pivotal role in not only shaping personal worship practices but also anchoring the collective religious ethos of the Muslim community.

Personal Connection with God:

In Islam, cultivating a personal connection with God begins with sincere and heartfelt worship. Prayers, supplications, and remembrance of God form the basis of this relationship, providing opportunities for believers to express their gratitude, seek guidance, and find solace in times of distress. Albeit structured, Islamic worship is designed to create a space for a direct and unfiltered communion with the Creator, emphasizing the importance of intention and sincerity in every act of worship.

Beyond prescribed acts of worship, the concept of 'dhikr' or remembrance of God lies at the core of nurturing a personal connection. Muslims are encouraged to engage in constant mindful remembrance of God throughout their daily lives, recognizing and appreciating the presence of the Divine in all facets of existence. This continuous mindfulness serves as a reminder of our dependence on God and reinforces the spiritual bond between the individual and the Almighty.

Self-reflection and contemplation also play a pivotal role in strengthening one's connection with God. The Quran, being the central religious text, offers wisdom and guidance, leading believers to introspect, seek understanding, and contemplate the signs of God's creation. Through deep reflection on the teachings of the Quran and the life of Prophet Muhammad (peace be upon him), individuals can cultivate a deeper awareness of their purpose and their relationship with the Creator.

Furthermore, acts of kindness, charity, and compassion towards fellow beings are intrinsic to developing a personal connection with God. Islam places great emphasis on social responsibility and the treatment of others, teaching that genuine love and mercy towards humanity are expressions of faith and devotion to God. By embodying these qualities, individuals not only fulfill their obligations to society but also deepen their connection with the Divine, recognizing the interconnectedness of all creations.

Chapter VI
PROPHETS AND ANGELS

Introduction to Divine Messengers:

Divine messengers are revered figures who serve as conduits for delivering the divine will and guidance to humanity. Stemming from various faith traditions, the belief in divine messengers underscores the interconnectedness of humanity with the transcendent realm. These messengers are often regarded as exemplars of virtue, morality, and spiritual insight, embodying the highest ideals of compassion, wisdom, and devotion. Their roles extend beyond mere conveyors of messages; they are entrusted with the monumental task of guiding and admonishing their respective communities towards righteousness and spiritual fulfillment.

Throughout history, these messengers have emerged at pivotal junctures to revive faith, impart ethical teachings, and steer communities away from moral decadence. Acknowledging their divine mission and unwavering commitment, believers uphold these figures as paragons of faith and obedience to the divine will. The narratives surrounding divine messengers enrich the tapestry of religious literature, offering lessons on resilience, steadfastness, and unwavering faith in the face of adversity.

The ethos of divine messengers is intrinsically linked to the notion of an overarching purpose in human existence, emphasizing the pursuit of spiritual enlightenment, moral rectitude, and communal solidarity. Their lives serve as exemplars of the vivid manifestation of faith in action, fostering resilience amid tribulations and inspiring hope in the promise of divine mercy. Delving into the nuances of their transformative impact on societies, one uncovers a tableau of moral transformation, societal reform, and spiritual revival catalyzed by the indelible influence of divine messengers. Through their teachings, these luminous figures illuminate the path toward communion with the divine, nurturing a collective consciousness rooted in humility, empathy, and reverence for all creation.

Angelic Beings and Their Purpose:

Angelic beings are believed to serve as intermediaries between the human realm and the divine realm, conveying important messages, offering protection, and guiding individuals towards spiritual enlightenment. The concept of angels transcends cultural and religious boundaries, appearing in Judaic, Christian, Islamic, and other faith systems, each with unique interpretations and roles.

In Islam, for example, angels are perceived as obedient servants of Allah, carrying out His commands without question. This unwavering loyalty and commitment distinguish them as beings of immense purity and righteousness. Reflecting on their purpose, one finds that angels embody symbolism, representing virtues such as purity, guidance, and mercy. Their presence is often associated with pivotal moments in religious history and personal spiritual experiences, signifying divine intervention and protection.

Moreover, stories and accounts of angelic encounters spark contemplation on the interconnectivity between the material and spiritual realms, prompting individuals to seek deeper understanding of their own existence and purpose. Understanding the nature of angelic beings also brings to light the concept of spiritual guardianship in various belief systems, instilling a sense of comfort and protection in the hearts of the faithful.

In the monotheistic Abrahamic traditions, such as Judaism, Christianity, and Islam, the role of angels in conveying divine messages and fulfilling divine mandates is paramount. In the Hebrew Bible, for instance, angelic visitations are portrayed as pivotal moments in shaping the destinies of individuals and nations. The appearance of angels to figures like Abraham, Jacob, and Daniel signifies the direct involvement of celestial entities in human affairs.

Similarly, the New Testament records multiple instances of angelic appearances, notably the Annunciation to Mary and the announcement of Christ's resurrection. These interactions underline the belief in angelic interventions as integral components of God's plan for humanity. In Islam, the Quran contains numerous references to angelic encounters, particularly in the revelations received by the Prophet Muhammad through Archangel Gabriel, reinforcing the concept of divine guidance facilitated by celestial entities.

Beyond the Abrahamic faiths, angelic interactions feature prominently in diverse cultural and religious contexts worldwide. Stories of divine messengers visiting and assisting individuals during crucial junctures are pervasive across various mythologies and folklore. The depiction of guardian angels, spiritual guides, and benevolent supernatural beings resonates deeply with the human longing for transcendence and divine protection.

While the nature of these interactions varies across different belief systems, a common thread emerges in the universal portrayal of angels as bearers of comfort, guidance, and divine decrees. The fascination with angelic encounters permeates art, literature, and popular culture, reflecting humanity's curiosity about the celestial realm and its influence on earthly affairs. The significance of these interactions between angels and humankind extends beyond religious dogma, offering insights into the intertwined relationship between the seen and unseen worlds.

Role of Prophets in Faith Tradition:

Prophets hold a revered position in the faith tradition, serving as intermediaries between the divine and humanity. Their significance lies not only in delivering messages from the divine realm but also in exemplifying moral conduct and righteous living. As messengers chosen by God, prophets are entrusted with the crucial task of guiding and enlightening human societies, fostering spiritual development, and steering individuals towards the path of righteousness.

In various religious traditions, prophets are venerated for their unwavering commitment to upholding justice, compassion, and ethical values. Their teachings transcend time and continue to inspire followers to this day. The impact of their guidance is evident in the influence of scriptures and teachings preserved over centuries, influencing the moral compass of entire civilizations.

Furthermore, prophets are often perceived as beacons of hope and mercy, embodying qualities that offer solace and direction during periods of adversity and uncertainty. Their exemplary lives serve as models for believers seeking to front on to existence with integrity and conviction. Through their words and deeds, prophets offer tangible demonstrations of faith in action, demonstrating the application of divine principles in daily life.

The role of prophets in faith tradition extends beyond individual salvation; it encompasses the broader objectives of societal reform, moral revival, and the cultivation of virtuous communities. Their pronouncements and actions reflect an unwavering commitment to social justice, equality, and the pursuit of harmony among diverse communities. They advocate for the marginalized, champion the cause of the oppressed, and strive to foster unity amidst diversity, thereby promoting a vision of inclusive coexistence.

Furthermore, the prophetic legacy serves as a testament to the continuity and coherence of divine guidance throughout history. From Adam to Muhammad, the succession of prophets underscores the cohesive nature of the divine message, reinforcing fundamental truths while adapting to the evolving needs of humanity. Each prophet, while distinct in their mission and community, contributes to the tapestry of divine guidance, collectively forming a comprehensive framework for spiritual fulfillment and moral rectitude.

The Sinai Revelation - Moses as a Paradigm Prophet:

Moses, revered in the Abrahamic faiths as a paradigm prophet, played a pivotal role in delivering the divine message and guiding the Children of Israel. Central to his story is the dramatic event known as the Sinai Revelation, where he received the Ten Commandments and established a covenant with God. This monumental encounter exemplifies the connection between humanity and the divine. The narrative of the Sinai Revelation not only holds immense spiritual significance but also embodies lessons for believers across generations. As the central figure in the Exodus story, Moses epitomizes unwavering faith, resilience, and ethical leadership. His journey from the oppression of Egypt to the revelation at Mount Sinai encapsulates the trials and triumphs integral to prophetic missions. The encounter at Mount Sinai stands as an archetype of divine communication, emphasizing the pivotal role of prophets as conduits for transmitting God's guidance to humankind. Furthermore, the teachings conveyed during the Sinai Revelation underscore the essential principles of monotheism, moral conduct, and social justice. The divine laws and ethical precepts bestowed upon Moses at Sinai continue to resonate within religious traditions and serve as foundational pillars for ethical living and communal harmony. Additionally, the covenant established at this momentous event reflects the eternal bond between God and His chosen messengers, solidifying the prophetic legacy as a source of spiritual enlightenment and ethical direction.

Prophet Muhammad - The Seal of the Prophets:

Prophet Muhammad occupies a paramount position as the final prophet in Islamic tradition. His exemplary character, ethical conduct, and unwavering dedication to spreading monotheism left an indelible mark on human history. Muhammad's mission began at the age of 40 with the initial revelation in the cave of Hira, which marked the commencement of his role as a prophet and messenger of God. Through his teachings and actions, he championed compassion, justice, and equality, thereby challenging prevalent social and economic injustices in pre-Islamic Arabian society. His leadership during periods of adversity and warfare showcased resilience, forgiveness, and mercy, inspiring generations to come. The significance of Prophet Muhammad as the Seal of the Prophets lies not only in his message but also in his embodiment of the divine principles he espoused. He served as a universal role model, demonstrating the application of spiritual guidance in diverse facets of life, including governance, family relations, and global harmony. From the Treaty of Medina to the Farewell Pilgrimage, his legacy encapsulates wisdom, diplomacy, and foresight, offering lessons for facing contemporary challenges. The impact of Prophet Muhammad is evident in the continued reverence and emulation of his character by Muslims worldwide, alongside scholarly endeavors to understand and disseminate his teachings. His teachings on compassion, tolerance, and knowledge continue to reverberate across cultural and geographical boundaries, fostering dialogue, mutual understanding, and ethical conduct. As the Seal of the Prophets, Prophet Muhammad signifies the culmination of a line of messengers while heralding a renewed era of human spirituality and moral compass.

Scriptural References and Teachings:

In the Islamic faith, the Quran serves as the ultimate source of guidance and wisdom, containing numerous references to the prophets and their pivotal roles in delivering the message of monotheism. As stated in Surah Al-An'am (6:84), "And We gave him Isaac and Jacob; each of them We guided, and before him, We guided Noah, and among his descendants David, Solomon, Job, Joseph, Moses, and Aaron. Thus do We reward the doers of good." These verses highlight the interconnectedness of prophethood and the continuity of divine guidance throughout history. The teachings attributed to the prophets emphasize moral conduct, compassion, social justice, and steadfast faith in the Almighty. Prophets such as Abraham, Moses, Jesus, and Muhammad, peace be upon them, are revered for their unwavering commitment to conveying the principles of righteousness and upholding the sanctity of human life. Their exemplary lives and teachings continue to inspire believers to lead virtuous and ethical lives, fostering harmony and goodwill within communities. Moreover, the Quran emphasizes the universality of prophethood, acknowledging that messengers were sent to every nation, speaking the language of their people and imparting divine guidance suited to their circumstances. This inclusivity underscores the overarching message of monotheism and underscores the interconnectedness of all prophetic missions, leading mankind towards a common understanding of spiritual truth. In addition to the Quranic references, Islamic tradition holds sacred the Hadith literature, which preserves the sayings and practices of Prophet Muhammad, serving as a complementary source of guidance.

Chapter VII
JUDGMENT DAY

The Trumpet Call:

As the culmination of time approaches, the trumpet call is an awe-inspiring event that marks the beginning of the end. Described as a deafening sound that will reverberate throughout the universe, the trumpet call serves as a universal signal to humanity, signaling the commencement of the Day of Judgment. The scriptures vividly describe this momentous occasion, portraying it as a clarion call that can shake mountains and instill fear into the hearts of all living beings. This divine signal will strike a chord in the hearts of humanity, awakening them from the slumber of heedlessness and signaling the onset of the apocalyptic events. The resounding call of the trumpet will disrupt the tranquility of the world, heralding the arrival of the reckoning and the culmination of human history. Moreover, the trumpet call is not merely a symbolic event; it holds immense significance in theological and eschatological traditions. According to the Islamic scriptures, the angel Israfil is entrusted with the duty of blowing the trumpet, an act that will unfold the next phase of existence. The repercussions of this celestial blast are far-reaching, as it will lead to the dissolution of the material world and pave the way for the unfolding of divine justice. The trumpet call serves as a solemn reminder of the transitory nature of worldly life, urging individuals to contemplate the purpose of their existence and prepare for the ultimate accountability before the Divine.

Resurrection:

In Islam, the concept of resurrection symbolizes the ultimate manifestation of God's justice and mercy, offering believers the opportunity for redemption and eternal bliss. The Quran vividly illustrates the process through which the dead will be resurrected, emphasizing the absolute power of Allah to revive every soul and gather humanity for the Day of Judgment. The belief in resurrection fuels the moral compass and ethical conduct of individuals, as they are conscious of being held accountable for their actions in both the worldly life and the hereafter.

The resurrection marks the culmination of human existence and serves as the bridge between temporal life and the everlasting realm. It signifies a transition from the physical slumber of death to the spiritual awakening of the soul, where all deeds, however inconspicuous, are brought to light. The Quran describes the resurrection as a solemn event, with the earth bearing witness to its transformation and celestial bodies concurring in a cosmic display of divine sovereignty.

Furthermore, the concept of resurrection instills a deep sense of accountability and vigilance, reminding believers that their earthly deeds have an everlasting impact and are subject to scrutiny on the Day of Reckoning. This awareness leads to a conscientious and righteous way of life, driven by the anticipation of standing before God and facing the consequences of one's choices.

Moreover, the Quran emphasizes the transformative nature of resurrection, highlighting that it is not merely a return to life but a complete renewal of the human condition. It signifies the shedding of imperfections, the resolution of injustices, and the attainment of true justice under the sovereignty of the Most Compassionate. The resurrection is the ultimate equalizer, granting every individual an equitable chance at redemption and salvation, irrespective of social status or worldly wealth.

The Gathering:

At the predetermined moment known only to the Divine, when the trumpet sounds and the earth trembles, all of humanity will be gathered before the Almighty for judgment. The chaos and tumult of this assembly will strike awe into the hearts of all souls, as they stand together in anticipation of their eternal fate. It is a moment that transcends time and space, as every individual, from the beginning of creation until the end of time, is summoned to stand before the Lord.

The gathering will encompass the righteous and the wicked, the pious and the rebellious, the humble and the arrogant. There will be no distinction of race, nationality, or social status, as all will be equal before the Absolute Majesty of God. The enormity of this congregation will reflect the diversity and vastness of the human experience, with every soul present to bear witness to its deeds and intentions.

The atmosphere will be charged with an electric sense of trepidation and solemnity, as each person contemplates the consequences of their actions and seeks solace in the mercy of the Most Merciful. The gathering will mark the ultimate convergence of human destiny, as the tapestry of individual lives unfolds into a collective narrative that testifies to the power and wisdom of the Creator.

Amidst this assembly, the weight of responsibility and accountability will rest heavy upon every soul. The gaze of the Almighty will penetrate the depths of the heart, laying bare the truth of each individual's character and conduct. There will be no refuge from the piercing scrutiny of divine justice, as the deeds of humans are laid bare and examined with absolute clarity and fairness.

The gathering will be a moment of reckoning, where the fleeting pleasures and distractions of worldly life will dissolve into insignificance. No veil or pretense will shield the true nature of humanity from the omniscient knowledge of the Creator. Every thought, word, and action will be accounted for, as the scales of justice weigh the moral worth of each soul.

Yet, amidst the gravity of this assembly, there is also an opportunity for redemption and salvation. The gathering serves as a catalyst for introspection and repentance, as individuals confront the reality of their transgressions and seek the forgiveness and mercy of God. It is a testament to the boundless compassion of the Almighty, who offers the chance for renewal and atonement in the face of human fallibility.

The Divine Ledger:

When it comes to the concept of judgment and accountability, the idea of a divine ledger becomes significant. The notion suggests a system that meticulously records every deed, action, intention, and thought undertaken by individuals throughout their lives. This celestial recording of deeds and actions reflects the absolute justice and fairness inherent in the divine paradigm. It encapsulates the embodiment of ultimate knowledge and awareness, encompassing the minutest details that shape human existence.

The divine ledger is not subject to error, omission, or manipulation. It stands as an indelible testimony to the moral and ethical conduct of every individual, immortalizing the record of their journey through life. Every act of kindness, every moment of patience, every instance of selfless sacrifice finds its place within this eternal archive, just as every transgression, each missed opportunity for righteousness, and all acts of malice are meticulously inscribed upon its pages.

The recording of deeds and actions in the divine ledger serves as an impartial reflection of one's choices and their consequences. It symbolizes the manifestation of absolute truth, unclouded by bias or prejudice. In this accounting, the scales of justice are perpetually upheld, ensuring that no aspect of one's existence escapes equitable consideration.

Furthermore, the divine ledger transcends the limitations of mortal memory and perception. It encompasses not only overt actions but also the intentions that drive them, granting significance to the essence of each individual's character. This holistic approach elucidates the breadth and depth of human responsibility and moral agency, providing a comprehensive insight into the fabric of human consciousness.

The understanding of the divine ledger compels contemplation on the nature of personal responsibility and the ramifications of individual choices. It underscores the intrinsic relationship between actions and their consequences, emphasizing the impact of one's conduct. The fidelity of the divine ledger signifies an eternal register, wherein the totality of one's existence is enshrined, immortalized in the annals of cosmic justice.

Scales of Justice:

In the cosmic scales of justice, every deed and action is meticulously weighed to determine its moral weight and ethical significance. The concept of divine justice envisions a celestial balance where the scales meticulously measure the righteousness and sins of each individual. This allegorical representation reflects the sense of accountability in the Islamic understanding of judgment. The scales of justice symbolize the meticulous examination of a person's deeds, assigning precise value and significance to every action and intention.

The Quran vividly describes the weighing of deeds on the Day of Judgment, portraying a scene where even the smallest good or evil act is not overlooked. The precision of this scale highlights the divine emphasis on fairness and equity in assessing the ethical conduct of humanity. Each soul's scrolls of deeds - their actions, intentions, and their impacts on others - are meticulously unfurled and placed on the scales, as the ultimate judgment awaits.

The symbolism of the scales also conveys the notion that divine justice transcends human limitations, acknowledging that every virtuous deed contributes to the universal harmony, while every transgression disrupts the balance. It encapsulates the idea that no act of goodness or wrongdoing goes unnoticed, and just recompense awaits every soul.

The spiritual significance of the scales of justice extends beyond mere measurement; it reflects the underlying belief in the ultimate triumph of righteousness over sin. The meticulous weighing serves as a reminder that the pursuit of virtues and the avoidance of sins carry implications for one's eternal destiny. Moreover, it emphasizes the principle of accountability, reinforcing the ethical responsibility of individuals towards themselves and others.

The scales of justice also serve as a catalyst for introspection and self-evaluation in the earthly realm. It compels individuals to reflect on their actions, motivating them to tread the path of righteousness and seek forgiveness for their transgressions. This awareness of spiritual accountability fosters moral rectitude, empathy, and compassion, instilling a deep sense of consciousness and mindfulness in people's interactions and choices.

Witnesses to Truth:

In the proceedings of Judgment Day, the gathering of all souls is witnessed not only by the Almighty but also by the prophets and angels. These messengers of God stand ready to testify to the truth of individuals' actions and intentions throughout their worldly lives. The testimonies of the prophets and angels serve as a crucial component in the divine reckoning, providing an impartial account of each soul's conduct and faith. As the assembly awaits its destiny, the voices of the prophets resound with unwavering certainty, recounting the deeds and dedication of humanity. Their testimonies are not only a validation of God's prescience but also a testimony to the individual's adherence or deviation from the path of righteousness. Each word spoken carries the weight of divine authority, affirming the integrity of the reckoning process.

Moreover, the angels bear witness to the unseen acts of devotion and transgression committed by every living being. Their presence underscores the omnipresence of God's knowledge, for nothing escapes their vigilant observation. They unfold the tapestry of human existence, illuminating concealed virtues and vices, revealing the sincerity or hypocrisy of each soul. The accounts presented by these celestial witnesses serve as an undeniable record of one's life, laying bare the innermost thoughts and deeds that define an individual's moral essence.

As such, the testimonies of the prophets and angels become an integral part of the judgment, guiding the determination of each soul's eternal fate. This divine scrutiny, illuminated by the testimonies of the venerable prophets and angels, encapsulates the gravity and accountability inherent in the final reckoning. It is a testament to the nature of divine justice, underpinned by the unassailable truthfulness of these celestial witnesses. Through their testimonies, the righteousness of the righteous is validated, and the relentlessness of evil is exposed, ensuring that every soul faces an equitable judgment Thus, in the presence of such eminent witnesses, the reality of one's spiritual standing is unveiled, and the individual is left to contemplate the implications of their life's narrative, poised between hope and apprehension as they await the ultimate decree.

The Reckoning:

As the Day of Judgment unfolds, every soul will undergo a reckoning of their deeds and beliefs. This is the moment of ultimate scrutiny, where no action, however minute, will escape divine justice. Each individual will be held accountable for their choices, actions, and intentions throughout their earthly existence. The infinite wisdom and mercy of the Almighty will ensure that every aspect of one's life is thoroughly examined.

In this stage of the reckoning, no veil will shield the reality of one's deeds. The balance of righteousness and sin will be meticulously weighed; not even an atom's weight of good will go unacknowledged, nor will any injustice remain unaddressed. Every act of kindness, every word spoken, and every thought harbored will be laid bare before the absolute truth, allowing no room for evasion or denial.

The consequences of this meticulous scrutiny will be capital. For those whose hearts were illuminated with faith, whose actions reflected righteousness and compassion, the reward will be a glorious abode in the gardens of Paradise. Their devoted worship, perseverance in trials, and acts of charity will have secured them eternal bounties and bliss in the presence of the Most Merciful.

Conversely, those who turned a blind eye to their moral responsibilities, engaged in oppression, and rejected the divine guidance will face the wrathful justice of the Day of Reckoning. The inevitable consequence of their defiance will be the tormenting inferno of Hellfire, where every moment brings agony and despair, an existence devoid of hope and comfort.

The severity of the consequences is not arbitrary but determined by the inherent justice of the Divine. Each individual's accountability is proportionate to their capabilities, circumstances, and knowledge. In this respect, equity prevails, as the Most Just Judge takes into account every nuance of a person's life, ensuring fairness and precision in the dispensation of justice.

The realization of this overwhelming accountability serves as a compelling reminder for believers to strive for excellence in character and conduct. This understanding should ignite within each soul a fervent determination to uphold righteousness, seek forgiveness for shortcomings, and express gratitude for the countless blessings bestowed upon them. The impending reckoning thus becomes a catalyst for virtuous actions, sincere repentance, and unwavering faith in the promise of divine mercy and justice.

Paradise and Hellfire:

The Quran vividly describes paradise (Jannah) as the ultimate abode of bliss for those who led a life of righteousness and piety. It is depicted as a garden of everlasting delight, where its inhabitants will experience boundless joy, serenity, and fulfillment. The Quranic descriptions of paradise appeal to all human senses, presenting it as a realm of eternal satisfaction and reward reserved for the virtuous believers. Conversely, hellfire (Jahannam) stands as the embodiment of divine retribution for those who turned away from the path of righteousness and succumbed to heedlessness and disobedience. Described in harrowing detail, hellfire represents an abode of suffering, anguish, and torment, serving as the destination for those who rejected the guidance of the Almighty. The Quran presents these contrasting destinies as a powerful reminder of the accountability and consequences that accompany human actions and choices. Each person's deeds will ultimately determine their eternal abode, reflecting the principle of divine justice upheld in the Quran. By emphasizing the reality of paradise and hellfire, the Quran compels individuals to reflect on their actions and strive for spiritual rectitude, reminding them of the implications of their decisions. This concept serves to instill a deep sense of responsibility and consciousness in every aspect of life, as individuals are urged to ponder the eternal consequences of their choices and conduct. Furthermore, the Quran consistently reaffirms the mercy and compassion of the Almighty, offering avenues for repentance, forgiveness, and redemption. Even amid the stark portrayal of hellfire, the Quran extends opportunities for atonement and salvation, underscoring the overarching message of divine mercy and compassion.

Chapter VIII
ETERNAL LIFE

The Paradise - A Realm of Eternal Bliss:

Descriptions of Paradise in the context of the afterlife often evoke images of idyllic landscapes, serene gardens, flowing rivers, and abundant fruits. These depictions are imbued with vivid colors, intoxicating fragrances, and an atmosphere of tranquility that transcends earthly experiences. The Quranic portrayal of Paradise is one of unparalleled beauty and perfection, offering a refuge of unending joy and fulfillment to the righteous. It emphasizes the tangible rewards awaiting those who lived a life of piety, generosity, and devotion to God. The descriptions underscore the concept of eternal bliss as a resplendent abode where inhabitants are adorned with luxurious garments and adorned with exquisite jewelry. The companionship of like-minded souls and the company of noble and pure beings further enrich the splendor of this celestial realm.

Beyond the physical delights, the Quran also speaks of spiritual pleasures awaiting the dwellers of Paradise. The verses expound upon the intimate communion with the Divine, where believers will bask in the effulgence of God's mercy and love. The presentation of Paradise is not merely an enticement for virtuous actions, but an affirmation of the ultimate justice and benevolence of God. It serves as a source of solace and hope, especially during times of adversity, inspiring individuals to strive for righteousness and perseverance.

Moreover, the imagery of Paradise in Islamic tradition extends beyond the sensory realm, encompassing intellectual and emotional fulfilment. It alludes to the absence of suffering, anxiety, and anguish, replaced by a state of contentment and harmony. The depiction of paradise symbolizes the culmination of human aspirations, where desires are met without deprivation or dissatisfaction. This vision of eternal bliss resonates deeply within the hearts of believers, cultivating a yearning for spiritual elevation and righteousness.

Hell - Consequences for the Unrighteous:

In Islamic theology, the concept of hell serves as a reminder of the consequences that await those who defy divine guidance and perpetuate evil. Descriptions of hell in the Quran paint a stark, uncompromising picture of the agony and torment awaiting the unrighteous. The Quran portrays hell as a place of searing flames, scorching winds, and boiling water, where punishment is meted out in accordance with the deeds of the inhabitants. The intensity and diversity of these punishments underscore the gravity of transgressions and the absolute justice of divine retribution.

Beyond the physical anguish, hell represents a state of utter despair and hopelessness. It is a bleak realm devoid of mercy, where the unrepentant face eternal separation from divine grace and blessings. The Quranic imagery invokes a chilling sense of loss and regret, underscoring the irreversible consequences of a life lived in defiance of moral principles and ethical obligations.

Moreover, hell serves as a powerful deterrent against wrongdoing, compelling believers to diligently adhere to virtuous conduct and strive for righteousness. The vivid depictions of hellfire and its agonizing punishments emphasize the critical importance of upholding moral integrity and avoiding transgressions that could lead to eternal damnation. This sobering portrayal instills a sense of accountability and mindfulness, steering individuals away from actions and attitudes that may incur divine wrath and condemnation.

The theological significance of hell extends beyond retribution, encapsulating the broader implications of human choice and responsibility. It underscores the inherent dualism of existence, wherein the exercise of free will determines one's ultimate destiny. By elucidating the dire consequences of straying from the path of righteousness, the concept of hell emphasizes the imperative of conscious and deliberate moral decision-making, reshaping behavior and attitudes in alignment with divine injunctions.

The Soul's Journey - From Death to Resurrection:

It is believed that upon death, the souls of the deceased enter a state known as the Barzakh, an intermediary realm where the souls experience a period of waiting and preparation for the Day of Judgment. In this transitional state, the souls of the righteous are said to experience peace and comfort, while the souls of the unrighteous endure torment and punishment. The Quran provides vivid descriptions of the events that unfold during this period, offering believers insight into the nature of the afterlife. Central to the concept of the soul's journey is the belief in resurrection, where every individual will be raised from the dead to face ultimate judgment before their Creator. The resurrection is viewed as a momentous event, marking the culmination of human existence and the beginning of eternal life. According to Islamic teachings, the resurrection will bring about a reckoning of each person's deeds, with divine justice prevailing for all. This belief serves as a powerful motivator for individuals to lead virtuous lives and remain mindful of their actions, knowing that they will be held to account in the hereafter. Additionally, the concept of resurrection underscores the idea of continuity and accountability beyond the confines of mortal life, reinforcing the importance of living in accordance with moral and ethical principles. The soul's journey from death to resurrection exemplifies the interconnectedness between the earthly realm and the hereafter, highlighting the eternal consequences of one's choices and actions. It serves as a reminder of the transitory nature of worldly life and the significance of spiritual striving. Ultimately, the belief in the soul's journey from death to resurrection instills hope, purpose, and commitment to a life of faith and virtue, anchoring believers in the anticipation of a meaningful and everlasting existence beyond the temporal confines of this world.

Intermediary State - The Barzakh Experience:

The concept of the Barzakh, also known as the Intermediary State, serves as the transitional period between earthly life and the Day of Resurrection, forming an essential aspect of the believer's journey into the afterlife. According to Islamic teachings, every individual who experiences death enters the Barzakh, which encompasses a state of waiting and preparation for the ultimate judgment. While the specific nature of this phase remains beyond human comprehension, Islamic scholars have sought to elucidate its significance through theological and mystical interpretations.

The Barzakh, often depicted as a realm of duality, represents a time of reflection and assessment. It is believed that during this phase, the soul undergoes a period of purification and accountability. This period is pivotal, as it offers individuals the chance to reconcile their deeds and seek forgiveness for any transgressions before facing their eternal destiny. The Qur'an and Hadith literature provide glimpses into the Barzakh experience, highlighting elements such as the questioning of the deceased by angelic figures and the soul's reunion with righteous companions as sources of comfort.

Moreover, the Barzakh is depicted as a space where the deceased remain cognizant of their earthly life and the loved ones they have left behind. While the exact nature of this awareness is shrouded in mystery, it underscores the connection between the temporal and spiritual realms. Furthermore, Islamic tradition emphasizes the role of prayers, charitable acts, and supplications offered on behalf of the deceased during the Barzakh, advocating for the continued impact of benevolent actions on the souls of the departed.

Throughout history, Islamic scholars have deliberated on the conceptual dimensions of the Barzakh, integrating philosophical, mystical, and ethical perspectives into their exegeses. Classical interpretations have explored the existential implications of the Intermediary State, emphasizing the interplay between the corporeal and ethereal aspects of human existence. Conversely, contemporary scholars have engaged with modern discourses to reexamine the relevance of the Barzakh within the context of evolving societal complexities and scientific inquiries.

Spiritual Preparation:

Spiritual preparation for the afterlife involves aligning one's values and actions with the eternal goals outlined by religious teachings. This process requires introspection, self-discipline, and a deep commitment to ethical living. The goal of preparing spiritually is to attain a sense of peace and fulfillment in this life, while also ensuring a positive outcome in the hereafter.

Central to spiritual preparation is the concept of mindfulness and intentionality in every action. Individuals are encouraged to live with purpose and to be mindful of their choices, ensuring that they align with the overarching moral and ethical principles taught by their faith. This may involve regular self-assessment and reflection on personal conduct, as well as seeking forgiveness for any wrongdoings.

Furthermore, spiritual preparation often emphasizes the development of virtuous qualities such as compassion, humility, and generosity. Practitioners strive to embody these virtues in their interactions with others, fostering harmonious relationships and community cohesion. Acts of charity and service become integral components of this spiritual preparation, as they demonstrate a commitment to social justice and the betterment of humanity at large.

In addition, adherents engage in the study and contemplation of sacred texts, seeking guidance and wisdom to inform their daily lives. This study may involve participation in religious rituals, meditation, and prayer, allowing individuals to deepen their connection to the divine and affirm their commitment to spiritual growth. Through these practices, believers aim to cultivate an awareness of the transcendent and to nurture a sense of reverence for the sacred.

Finally, spiritual preparation necessitates a steadfast dedication to moral integrity and ethical conduct in all aspects of life. By upholding honesty, fairness, and integrity in personal and professional endeavors, individuals demonstrate their commitment to living in accordance with the values of their faith. Moreover, ethical behavior extends to the treatment of others, promoting respect for human dignity and the inherent worth of all individuals.

Sumptuous Rewards - The Righteous' Just Deserts:

For the faithful adherents of Islam, the concept of 'Sumptuous Rewards' serves as a radiant beacon of hope and aspiration. Imagery permeates the descriptions of these rewards, conjuring up sumptuous visions of opulent gardens, cool shaded streams, and delectable fruits that are every bit as tantalizing as they are spiritually uplifting. The Quran paints a vision of Edenic delights awaiting the righteous, with promises of unbounding pleasure and eternal bliss for those who upheld piety in their worldly lives.

The sumptuous rewards reserved for the virtuous souls extend beyond mere sensory indulgences; they embody a spiritual elevation and a sense of unreserved contentment. The lavish paradisiacal surroundings are but a manifestation of the favor and grace bestowed upon the righteous, whose unwavering devotion and moral rectitude have endeared them to the Divine. Their reward includes not only the splendors of the physical realm but also the unparalleled joy of proximity to the Creator, basking in the glow of His benevolence and wisdom.

Embedded within the concept of 'Sumptuous Rewards' is the message of equity and justice, wherein the righteous are justly compensated for their steadfastness and commitment to the divine path. It serves as a testament to the belief that no act of goodness, however obscure, goes unnoticed or unrewarded by the Merciful. The sumptuous rewards are the ultimate affirmation of the bond between the Creator and the created, where acts of faith and virtue are met with unbounded munificence.

It is important to emphasize that the allure of these rewards isn't designed to be a mere gratification for earthly obedience, but rather an encouragement to pursue righteousness and integrity in all facets of life. These sumptuous rewards serve as a source of solace and motivation for believers, assuring them that their earthly struggles and sacrifices are not in vain, and that they resonate in an immortal realm where the pious are honored.

Eternal Companionship - Fellowship In the Hereafter:

It is believed that those who lead a righteous life will be rewarded with the company of loved ones and like-minded individuals in paradise. The Quran describes the joyous reunions awaiting the believers in the afterlife, emphasizing the eternal bond and unity that transcends earthly limitations.

The idea of eternal companionship provides a source of solace and inspiration for the faithful. It instills hope and fortitude in facing the trials of worldly life, knowing that the ultimate abode promises reunion with cherished souls. The concept underscores the importance of nurturing strong bonds based on faith, mutual respect, and genuine affection, as these connections will endure beyond the transience of mortal existence.

Moreover, the notion of fellowship in the hereafter serves as a reminder of the interconnectedness of humanity. It reflects the divine mercy and compassion that extend to all believers, offering a sense of belonging and community that transcends cultural, ethnic, and social boundaries. The Quranic verses beautifully illustrate the scenes of believers enjoying each other's company in the gardens of paradise, experiencing pure joy and fulfillment through their spiritual connections.

Additionally, the concept of eternal companionship carries implications for ethical conduct and interpersonal relationships in the present life. It encourages individuals to strive for harmonious interactions, empathy, and understanding, recognizing the value of nurturing wholesome connections that can endure beyond the confines of this world. This understanding motivates believers to uphold virtuous behavior and maintain steadfast integrity in all dealings, fostering an environment of mutual support and camaraderie.

Furthermore, the prospect of eternal companionship amplifies the significance of forgiveness, reconciliation, and compassion. It inspires individuals to seek resolution and harmony in their relationships, understanding the impact of their actions on the eternal bond with others. By prioritizing forgiveness and empathy, one paves the way for a future of everlasting fellowship and unity, embodying the values of compassion and kindness that are essential for spiritual growth and fulfillment.

The Vision of God and Ultimate Union:

According to Quran and Hadith, the vision of God represents the pinnacle of spiritual fulfillment, where the faithful believers are granted the privilege of beholding the divine countenance and experiencing a sense of proximity and intimacy with the Creator. While the human mind may struggle to comprehend the full magnitude of such an experience, it is described as a state of unparalleled joy, tranquility, and ecstasy.

The Quranic verses offer vivid descriptions of this blessed encounter, highlighting the radiance, beauty, and majesty of God as perceived by those who attain this honor. It is a union that transcends all earthly pleasures and fulfills the soul's deepest yearnings. Moreover, it serves as the culmination of a lifetime dedicated to faith, righteousness, and submission to the will of God. The anticipation of this sacred communion serves as a source of motivation and inspiration for believers, guiding their actions and shaping their attitudes towards life's challenges.

The doctrine of ultimate union also underscores the justice and mercy of God, as it represents the eternal reward for those who pursued virtue and remained steadfast in their devotion despite adversity. Furthermore, it instills a sense of hope and optimism in the face of worldly trials and tribulations, reminding believers that the transient nature of earthly existence is but a prelude to the everlasting bliss of the hereafter.

From a spiritual perspective, the pursuit of closeness to God forms the essence of worship and righteous living. It entails cultivating a deep, personal connection with the divine through prayer, remembrance, and conscious mindfulness of God's presence. This inner journey fosters a heightened awareness of the divine attributes and fosters a love for the Creator that becomes the driving force behind every action and intention. The vision of God and the promise of ultimate union serve as the beacon that illuminates the path of the faithful, guiding them through mortal life towards the abode of eternal peace and felicity.

Embracing this reality inspires believers to strive for moral excellence, to seek forgiveness for their shortcomings, and to extend compassion and kindness to others, recognizing that the rewards of paradise await those who remain steadfast in their beliefs and actions. As such, the aspiration for divine nearness and ultimate union shapes every facet of a believer's existence, infusing their daily lives with purpose, meaning, and a sense of spiritual connectedness.

Chapter IX
ETHICAL CONDUCT

Compassion, Honesty, and Integrity:

In the quest for ethical conduct, the cultivation of virtues plays a pivotal role in shaping individual character and societal harmony. Compassion stands as a foundational virtue, emphasizing empathy and understanding towards others' hardships and struggles. It involves actively seeking ways to alleviate suffering and contribute to the well-being of those in need. This empathy-driven approach extends beyond surface-level gestures and delves into the genuine desire to make a positive impact, reflecting the core essence of compassion. Moreover, honesty serves as a cornerstone of ethical behavior, fostering trust and transparency in all interactions. Upholding truthfulness in thoughts, words, and actions not only fortifies personal integrity but also strengthens the communal fabric by establishing a culture of reliability and accountability. Furthermore, integrity, intertwined with honesty, entails steadfast adherence to moral and ethical principles, even in the face of adversity. It exemplifies the unwavering commitment to upholding righteous values and staying true to one's convictions despite external pressures. The cultivation of these virtues requires continuous introspection, self-discipline, and a genuine willingness to embody these qualities in everyday life. As individuals embrace and nurture these virtues, they contribute to the creation of a virtuous society characterized by empathy, truth, and moral strength. Through the conscientious cultivation of compassion, honesty, and integrity, individuals become beacons of ethical conduct, inspiring others to follow suit and creating a ripple effect of positive change in their communities and beyond.

Condemnation of Evil:

Condemning evil requires a heightened sense of moral awareness and an unwavering commitment to uphold righteousness. It necessitates a deep understanding of the principles of justice, fairness, and compassion. It compels individuals to stand against oppression, corruption, and immorality in all spheres of life. The recognition of evil often stems from an acute awareness of societal injustices, discrimination, and violations of human rights, prompting individuals to advocate for positive change and stand as pillars of moral rectitude.

Resisting wrongdoings demands courage and resilience in the face of adversity. Individuals are called upon to challenge systemic injustices and confront unethical behavior with unwavering determination. Such moral fortitude is grounded in the principles espoused by the Quran, emphasizing the importance of standing up for truth and justice, even when faced with formidable opposition. This necessitates both personal and collective action to combat injustice and promote a more ethical and equitable society.

Recognizing and resisting evil also entails self-reflection and introspection. It requires individuals to constantly assess their own actions and beliefs, ensuring that they align with virtuous conduct and ethical standards. By fostering a culture of accountability and introspective scrutiny, one can contribute to the cultivation of a more morally conscious and principled society.

Furthermore, the condemnation of evil must be paired with efforts to reform and rehabilitate those who have succumbed to wrongdoing. While holding wrongdoers accountable, it is vital to recognize the potential for redemption and the capacity for positive change. This compassionate approach allows for the possibility of rehabilitation and reformation, emphasizing the intrinsic value of every individual and their potential for good.

The Role of Intention in Moral Decisions:

At the core of ethical decision-making lies the concept of 'niyyah' or intention in Islam. According to Islamic teachings, the Prophet Muhammad emphasized the importance of pure intentions in guiding one's conduct. The intention behind an action is believed to be the crucial factor that shapes its moral worthiness, transcending the external appearance of the deed. This principle underscores the depth of consciousness and sincerity required in aligning one's intentions with moral conduct, invoking a sense of mindfulness and self-awareness in individuals. It underscores the depth of awareness and accountability instilled within the ethical framework of Islam, reinforcing the notion that genuine intentions are integral to righteous actions. Whether in personal relationships, professional endeavors, or societal engagements, the purity of intentions offers a guiding light toward ethical propriety.

Exploring the broader philosophical discourse on intentionality, scholars across diverse ethical traditions have delved into the interplay between intentions and moral agency. The renowned philosopher Immanuel Kant expounded upon the inherent value of goodwill and the rational basis of moral intentions in his deontological ethics. Kant's emphasis on the categorical imperative highlights the imperative nature of directing intentions toward moral duties, advocating for a universal standard of ethical conduct rooted in the purity of intentions. Concurrently, virtue ethics elucidates the cultivation of moral character through habitual good intentions, nurturing the development of a virtuous ethical disposition. This multifaceted exploration of intentions in moral decisions underscores the pervasive influence of conscious motivations on individual and collective ethical conduct.

Moreover, the understanding of intention in moral decisions extends beyond the realm of individual actions, permeating the broader societal landscape and organizational paradigms. The formulation of ethical codes of conduct and professional standards hinges on the recognition of noble intentions as the bedrock of ethical integrity, safeguarding against ethical lapses and moral transgressions. In contemporary debates on corporate social responsibility and environmental stewardship, the ethical dimensions of intentions shape the ethical compass of businesses and institutions, accentuating the imperative of conscientious intent in cultivating socially responsible practices. Society at large is thus propelled toward fostering a culture where benevolent intentions underpin ethical decisions, serving as a beacon for harmonious coexistence and collective flourishing.

Chapter X
CALLS TO WORSHIP AND WARNINGS OF JUDGMENT

The Call to Worship - Embracing Divine Grace:

In the heart of every human being lies an innate yearning for connection with the divine. This call to worship, deeply rooted in the fabric of our existence, is a testament to the boundless grace that envelops humanity. It transcends borders and cultures, speaking to the universal nature of human spirituality. The act of worship, in all its forms, serves as a conduit through which individuals can express their gratitude, seek solace, and find purpose. Whether it takes the form of prayer, meditation, or acts of devotion, the call to worship beckons individuals to embrace a higher power, acknowledging the divine grace that sustains life. Recognizing this call as a manifestation of divine benevolence is paramount, for it illuminates the path to spiritual fulfillment and inner peace. By answering this call, individuals open themselves to experiences of transcendence and unity with the cosmos. This harmonious relationship with the divine not only enriches personal lives but also fosters a sense of interconnectedness with the world. The significance of this call to worship in human life cannot be overstated. It is in these moments of communion with the divine that individuals find solace amidst adversity, draw strength in times of uncertainty, and cultivate resilience in the face of challenges. Through worship, people discover a sense of belonging, anchoring themselves in a greater narrative that spans the boundaries of time and space. Moreover, the call to worship nurtures a sense of moral responsibility, guiding individuals towards compassion, empathy, and altruism. It instills a reverence for creation and prompts conscientious stewardship of the earth. Consequently, embracing the call to worship is not merely an act of personal devotion; rather, it is a catalyst for positive transformation within oneself and society at large.

As individuals heed this call, they become agents of positive change, striving to create a world imbued with justice, harmony, and peace. The universality of the call to worship underscores its capacity to bridge differences and unify diverse communities under the banner of shared spiritual experience. In a world often beset by discord, the call to worship stands as a unifying force, offering solace and hope to all who answer its summons.

The Importance of Prayer - Connection with the Divine:

Prayer holds a pivotal role in the life of a believer, serving as the means by which one maintains a direct connection with the divine. It stands as a sacred act through which individuals express gratitude, seek guidance, and find solace in times of distress. The act of prayer transcends mere recitation; it cultivates a sense of spiritual intimacy and fosters a deep bond with the Almighty. Through the rhythmic recitation of verses and supplications, individuals establish a communion with the divine presence, reflecting on their actions, seeking forgiveness, and meditating on the mercy that envelopes them. Prayer is a time for introspection, a period to realign one's soul with the values of righteousness and compassion. It serves as a reminder of the ephemeral nature of worldly pursuits and the essence of faith. Engaging in prayer not only fortifies the individual but also nurtures a sense of belonging within the broader community of believers. The collective act of congregational prayers unites individuals under the common banner of faith, reinforcing a shared commitment to righteousness and acknowledging the universal presence of the divine. Furthermore, prayer instills discipline and humility, guiding individuals to embody virtues of patience, perseverance, and humility. It reminds believers of their intrinsic dependence on the divine, fostering an unyielding reliance on God's providence. Through prostration and earnest supplication, the heart finds tranquility, and the mind attains clarity. Each prayer is a reaffirmation of one's faith, an acknowledgment of the omnipotence of the Creator, and a testimony of one's unwavering devotion. In essence, the act of prayer is not confined to a mere ritual but represents a sacred journey of self-discovery and spiritual elevation, serving as the cornerstone of a believer's relationship with the divine.

Warnings from Scripture:

Scripture holds invaluable lessons for believers, serving as a guide for ethical conduct, spiritual growth, and warnings of deviation. The Quran narrates stories of previous nations and their disregard for divine guidance, emphasizing the consequences of straying from the path of righteousness. Through these cautionary tales, readers are urged to contemplate the outcomes of disobedience and heed the wisdom imparted within the pages of sacred texts. The stories of past nations serve as reflections of human tendencies and serve as reminders that adherence to moral principles is essential for both individual and collective wellbeing. By examining historical accounts delineated in religious scriptures, individuals gain insights into the patterns of human behavior and the recurring themes of arrogance, defiance, and eventual downfall. These cautionary narratives inspire introspection and emphasize the significance of humility, gratitude, and obedience to the Divine. Moreover, they highlight the cyclical nature of societal rise and decline, shedding light on the inherent vulnerabilities of civilizations that deviate from righteousness. Engraved within these narratives are the consequences of neglecting moral virtues, disdain for fellow beings, and an unwillingness to embrace divine guidance. Through mindful reflection on these warnings from scripture, believers are called to uphold ethical standards, seek repentance for transgressions, and strive towards a righteous existence. The guidance provided by these cautionary tales extends beyond mere storytelling; it imparts messages aimed at cultivating virtue, fostering compassion, and preventing the repetition of historical errors. Therefore, the inclusion of these warnings from scripture serves as a reminder of the continuous struggle between good and evil, and the relevance of ethical conduct in shaping individual destinies and influencing the fate of communities.

Invitation to others:

Sharing the path to righteousness is not merely a duty but a privilege for those who have embraced the teachings of faith. Inviting others to the righteous way involves embodying the values and principles that one espouses, demonstrating through words and actions the beauty and fulfillment that faith brings to one's life. It entails extending a genuine invitation, rooted in sincerity and compassion, without imposition or judgment. This invitation should be an open-hearted offering of guidance and support, understanding that each individual's journey towards righteousness is unique. It requires patience, empathy, and a deep respect for others' beliefs and perspectives. As messengers of faith, it is imperative to communicate with humility and gentleness, striving to build bridges of understanding rather than walls of division. The approach should reflect an unwavering commitment to kindness and tolerance, allowing others the freedom to explore and inquire without fear of censure. At the core of this invitation lies the recognition of the inherent dignity of every individual, regardless of their current spiritual stance. It is a call to recognizing the shared humanity and the potential for spiritual growth within each person. Recipients of this invitation should feel uplifted and inspired by the genuine care and concern that underpin the message, finding solace in the embrace of a community that offers warmth, acceptance, and an authentic sense of belonging. Ultimately, the act of inviting others to righteousness extends beyond proselytizing; it is a gesture of goodwill, aimed at fostering a space where mutual understanding and harmony can flourish.

The Role of Community:

Community plays a pivotal role in fostering spiritual growth and creating a supportive environment for individuals to deepen their faith. Through collective worship, believers come together to strengthen their bonds and form a sense of unity within the community. This unity is not only essential for individual well-being but also contributes to the overall harmony and prosperity of society. The essence of communal worship lies in its ability to instill a sense of belonging and interconnectedness among its members. As worshippers gather in mosques, churches, synagogues, or temples, they partake in shared rituals and practices that reinforce their commitment to their beliefs.

One of the most significant aspects of community worship is the opportunity for individuals to learn from one another. Congregational gatherings provide a platform for mentorship, guidance, and mutual support, enabling both seasoned followers and newcomers to engage in meaningful discussions about faith. Furthermore, the act of praying together cultivates an atmosphere of empathy, compassion, and understanding, which strengthens the fabric of the community. Whether it is through joint recitations, sermons, or religious study groups, the exchange of knowledge and experiences within the community fosters spiritual enrichment and personal development.

Moreover, the solidarity experienced during congregational worship accentuates the significance of communal accountability. Believers hold each other responsible for upholding the ethical principles and moral values embedded within their faith tradition. This reciprocal obligation fosters a culture of integrity and conscientiousness, reinforcing the commitment to righteous conduct both inside and outside the sacred spaces. As individuals witness the dedication and sincerity of their peers, they are inspired to maintain their own spiritual journey with diligence and steadfastness.

The bond forged through communal worship extends beyond the confines of religious gatherings and permeates various facets of communal life. It enhances social cohesion, promotes collaboration in charitable endeavors, and provides a network of support during times of adversity. Additionally, the communal environment nurtures an inclusive ethos, welcoming people from diverse backgrounds and fostering an atmosphere of acceptance and understanding. Through fostering a sense of belonging and inclusivity, collective worship becomes a cornerstone for promoting peace, harmony, and tolerance within the wider society.

Chapter XI
SOCIAL RESPONSIBILITIES

The Role of Family in Society:

Families form the bedrock of any society, serving as the fundamental unit where values, social norms, and traditions are cultivated and passed down through generations. The family unit provides a nurturing environment for individuals to learn essential life skills, moral principles, and social responsibilities. In the context of the Quran's teachings, the family is considered a sanctuary, a place where love, respect, and compassion are fostered. It is within the family that individuals first experience the importance of empathy, cooperation, and mutual support. Moreover, families play a crucial role in shaping the emotional and psychological well-being of their members. They provide a sense of security, stability, and belonging, which are vital for the overall development of individuals. Furthermore, the family unit serves as a mechanism for socialization, preparing individuals to interact effectively within the wider society. Through familial interactions, individuals learn the art of compromise, conflict resolution, and interpersonal communication, which are essential for harmonious coexistence in communities. Additionally, families contribute to the preservation of cultural heritage and traditions. They serve as the primary vessels through which language, customs, and rituals are upheld and transmitted to future generations, ensuring the continuity of a society's identity. It is through family bonds that individuals gain a deep appreciation for their roots and heritage, fostering a sense of connection to their community and history. The Quran underscores the significance of upholding family values and maintaining strong familial ties, emphasizing the virtues of compassion, loyalty, and responsibility towards one's kin. As such, the family is not only an integral component of individual identity but also a cornerstone of societal cohesion and resilience.

Reverence for Parents and Elders:

Reverence for parents and elders encompasses not only the demonstration of courteous behavior but also the recognition and appreciation of the wisdom and experiences they have gathered throughout their lives. It entails displaying gratitude for the sacrifices made by parents and acknowledging the invaluable guidance provided by elders. Cultivating a culture of filial piety and venerating the elderly engenders a nurturing environment that values intergenerational knowledge exchange and fosters empathy and compassion within society. Moreover, honoring parents and elders is intrinsically linked to spiritual growth and attaining divine blessings. The Quran underscores the injunction to show kindness and humility towards parents, even if they happen to follow a different faith or hold divergent beliefs. This notion underlines the universality of the principle of filial piety and sorely highlights its relevance in the contemporary world. In contemporary societies, the preservation of the tradition of respecting parents and elders faces challenges due to shifting cultural dynamics and evolving family structures. Despite these transformations, the core values of filial piety continue to resonate and act as a moral compass for ensuring familial and societal well-being.

Community Cohesion:

According to the Quran, fostering community cohesion emphasizes the importance of working together harmoniously to achieve common objectives while preserving individual dignity and diversity. This unity is not merely about coexistence but about actively engaging in efforts to understand, support, and uplift one another. Central to fostering community cohesion is the notion of selflessness and putting the well-being of others above personal gain. It involves creating spaces for open dialogue and collaboration, allowing everyone to contribute their unique perspectives and abilities.

The Quran encourages believers to build cohesive communities by promoting empathy, compassion, and understanding among its members. This entails recognizing and valuing the contributions of individuals from various backgrounds, beliefs, and abilities, cultivating a society where all voices are heard and respected. Fostering community cohesion also involves embracing proactive measures to alleviate social disparities and injustices within the community. This can manifest through initiatives aimed at eradicating poverty, providing equal opportunities for education and employment, and ensuring access to healthcare for all members. Additionally, it involves upholding principles of justice and fairness to ensure that every individual feels secure and validated within the communal framework.

On the other hand, community cohesion extends beyond human interactions to encompass the environment and all living beings. Respecting the natural world and its inhabitants is integral to fostering harmony within the community, advocating for sustainable practices and ethical treatment of the ecosystem. By acknowledging the interconnectedness of all life forms, communities can strive towards ecological responsibility and stewardship, safeguarding the planet for future generations. Ultimately, fostering community cohesion aligns with the Quranic vision of a society built on solidarity, justice, and compassion, where every member is valued and supported.

Respecting All Forms of Life:

Respecting all forms of life conveys the message of compassion, empathy, and responsibility towards all living beings, whether human, animal, or plant. The Quran emphasizes that every form of life has intrinsic value and must be treated with dignity and care. This principle extends beyond the human species and urges believers to be mindful of their impact on the environment and the balance of the ecosystem. The concept of 'amanah' (trust) is central to this understanding, as humans are entrusted with the stewardship of the Earth and its inhabitants. With this trust comes the obligation to safeguard and nurture the natural world.

Furthermore, the Quran emphasizes the interconnectedness of all life forms and highlights the significance of maintaining harmony and equilibrium in the grand tapestry of creation. It asserts that the welfare of one species is intertwined with the welfare of others, emphasizing the interdependence and mutual responsibility shared among diverse life forms. The Quran provides guiding principles for humane treatment of animals, promoting kindness, and prohibiting cruelty. It highlights the ethical treatment of animals, including providing them with proper sustenance, shelter, and protection from harm. Furthermore, it advocates for the sustainable use of natural resources, cautioning against wastefulness and exploitation.

The Quran encourages believers to reflect upon the signs of nature, fostering an appreciation for the beauty and order in the natural world. By recognizing the design and diversity of creation, individuals are encouraged to develop a sense of awe and reverence for the magnificence of God's handiwork. This deep-seated respect for all forms of life serves as a guiding principle for ethical conduct, reinforcing the interconnectedness between humanity and the wider natural world. Through acknowledging the sanctity of life in all its manifestations, individuals are instilled with a sense of duty to protect and preserve the environment, whilst also nurturing a more compassionate and empathetic society.

Chapter XII
THE FASTING OF RAMADAN

The origins of Ramadan can be traced back to the revelation of the Quran to the Prophet Muhammad. It was during the month of Ramadan that the first verses of the Quran were revealed to the Prophet, marking it as a time of great spiritual significance and divine revelation for Muslims. This pivotal event solidified the sanctity of Ramadan and established it as a month of heightened spirituality and devotion.

Throughout Islamic history, the observance of Ramadan has evolved and deepened in significance. The early Muslim community, under the guidance of the Prophet Muhammad, embraced the fasting month as a means of purifying the soul, seeking closeness to God, and cultivating self-discipline. The practice of fasting from dawn until dusk during Ramadan became a cornerstone of Islamic worship, emphasizing restraint, empathy for the less fortunate, and spiritual reflection.

As Islamic civilization flourished, Ramadan became entrenched in the cultural and religious fabric of Muslim societies, influencing art, literature, and community life. The spiritual significance of Ramadan expanded beyond personal piety to encompass communal solidarity, compassion, and charitable acts. The fast-breaking meal, known as iftar, became a symbol of hospitality and shared blessings, fostering bonds of kinship and generosity among Muslims.

Moreover, Ramadan also holds historical importance in the realm of Islamic conquests and scholarship. It witnessed significant events such as Muslim victories and the contributions of scholars and intellectuals to Islamic thought and culture. The transformative impact of Ramadan on the Muslim world is evident in the diverse ways in which it has shaped the spiritual, intellectual, and social landscape of Islamic civilization.

In contemporary times, the observance of Ramadan continues to resonate deeply with Muslims worldwide, reflecting the historical legacy of this sacred month, and encapsulating the rich tapestry of Islamic history, spirituality, and cultural heritage.

The Spiritual Significance of Fasting:

Beyond its physical abstinence from food, drink, and other worldly pleasures from dawn until sunset, fasting is a deeply personal and communal act of worship that transcends the material realm. This act of self-discipline and sacrifice serves as a means of spiritual purification, renewal, and heightened awareness of one's connection with the divine. The elevated consciousness attained through fasting allows individuals to cultivate empathy for those less fortunate, fostering compassion and solidarity within the larger community.

The spiritual significance of fasting extends beyond the individual, creating an atmosphere of collective devotion and shared faith experiences. It serves as a unifying force that brings the global Muslim community together in a common purpose, strengthening bonds and reinforcing a sense of belonging. Through the shared commitment to fasting, individuals are encouraged to reflect on their relationship with God, seeking forgiveness, guidance, and inner peace. Moreover, fasting encourages contemplation and introspection, enabling adherents to focus on their spiritual growth, moral development, and ethical conduct.

From a theological perspective, fasting represents obedience to divine commandments and an opportunity to draw closer to God. It symbolizes the submission of one's desires and ego to the will of God, demonstrating an expression of faith and devotion. By embracing the discipline of fasting, individuals are reminded of the transient nature of worldly pleasures and the greater spiritual purpose underlying human existence. Fasting cultivates humility, gratitude, and a heightened sense of spiritual awareness, leading to a deepened understanding of faith and the pursuit of righteousness.

Furthermore, the spiritual significance of fasting is linked to the concept of self-restraint and self-improvement. By exercising restraint over physical desires, adherents strive to attain higher moral virtues and strengthen their spiritual resolve. Fasting instills perseverance, patience, and resilience, serving as a means of spiritual training to overcome life's challenges and temptations. It fosters a sense of self-mastery and control over base instincts, encouraging the development of virtuous character traits and a disciplined approach to life's trials. In essence, fasting becomes a transformative spiritual journey, fostering inner strength, self-awareness, and a deeper connection with the divine.

Islamic Jurisprudence on Fasting:

Islamic jurisprudence on fasting is rooted in the fundamental principles of Islamic law, known as Sharia. Fasting during the holy month of Ramadan is one of the Five Pillars of Islam and is a mandatory practice for all adult Muslims, with certain exceptions. The legal framework surrounding fasting encompasses various aspects, including the conditions for its obligation, the rules to be followed during fasting, and the consequences of non-observance. Islamic scholars derive these regulations from the Quran, Hadith (sayings and actions of Prophet Muhammad), and consensus among scholars. One of the essential concepts within Islamic jurisprudence regarding fasting is the intention (niyyah) to fast, which requires a person to make a conscious decision to fast before the start of each day's fast. This intention distinguishes acts of worship from ordinary acts and establishes the sincerity of the individual's devotion. Another critical element in the legal framework is the validation of the fast, which includes refraining from engaging in behaviors that nullify the fast, such as eating, drinking, smoking, and sexual activity, from dawn until sunset. Additionally, individuals who are menstruating, pregnant, nursing, ill, travelling, or elderly may be exempt from fasting, but they are required to make up for missed fasts at a later time or provide meals for the poor instead, depending on their specific circumstances. Furthermore, Islamic jurisprudence allows for flexibility in the form of fidya (compensation) or kaffara (expiation) for those unable to fast due to health reasons or other valid excuses. Fidya involves feeding a needy person for each day of missed fasting, while kaffara entails fasting for a specified number of days or providing food to the needy in addition to making up for the missed fasts. The legal framework also addresses the observance of Laylat al-Qadr, the Night of Decree, which holds immense significance during the last ten days of Ramadan. Scholarly interpretations guide Muslims on how to maximize their devotion and seek the blessings of this auspicious night.

Preparation for the Holy Month:

Preparation for the holy month of Ramadan is not merely a matter of abstaining from food and drink during daylight hours; it is a comprehensive spiritual and physical readiness for the unique and blessed time ahead. As the sacred month approaches, Muslims engage in various forms of preparation to maximize the benefits of Ramadan. This preparation encompasses mental, physical, and emotional components that collectively pave the way for a transformative experience.

One crucial aspect of preparing for Ramadan is the spiritual mindset. Believers seek to cleanse their hearts and minds, shedding negative traits and attitudes, while cultivating patience, compassion, and mindfulness. They engage in increased acts of worship, seeking forgiveness and blessings from the Almighty, and striving to purify their intentions for the upcoming fast. The process involves reflections on personal conduct, seeking self-improvement, and deepening one's connection with God through extra prayers and devotion.

Moreover, physical readiness for Ramadan entails taking proactive steps to ensure one's body and health are prepared for the rigors of fasting. This involves adopting a nutritious and balanced diet, gradually adjusting meal portions and timings to align with the prescribed fasting hours. Concurrently, regular exercise and sufficient rest are emphasized to maintain vitality throughout the month. In addition, medical consultations may be sought by individuals with specific health concerns in order to effectively manage any impacts of fasting on their well-being.

Emotionally, individuals strive to cultivate a sense of anticipation and eagerness for the approaching month. The anticipation of virtue, increased rewards, and divine mercy motivates and uplifts the spirits, fostering a positive outlook towards fasting and the spiritual journey that lies ahead. This emotional preparation also involves mental fortitude, as adherents aim to develop resilience and determination to overcome challenges and make the most of this special time.

Daily Rituals and Practices during Ramadan:

During the sacred month of Ramadan, Muslims engage in various daily rituals and practices as part of their observance of this holy period. The most significant ritual during Ramadan is the act of fasting, which involves abstaining from food, drink, smoking, and intimate relations from dawn until sunset. This physical discipline serves as a means of spiritual purification, self-discipline, and empathy for those less fortunate. The pre-dawn meal, known as Suhoor, is consumed before the Fajr (dawn) prayer, and the fast is broken with the Iftar meal at sunset, often with dates and water followed by a full meal. The act of breaking the fast is typically shared with family and community members, reinforcing the sense of unity and solidarity. Alongside fasting, engaging in increased acts of worship and devotion is encouraged throughout the month. Muslims are encouraged to read and reflect upon the Quran, perform additional prayers, and engage in charitable activities. The nights of Ramadan are particularly special, with many Muslims observing Taraweeh prayers at the mosque, listening to recitations of the Quran, and seeking divine guidance through prolonged supplications. Additionally, specific days within Ramadan hold particular significance. Laylat al-Qadr, also known as the Night of Decree, is believed to be the night when the Quran was first revealed to Prophet Muhammad and is thus considered the holiest night of the year. Many devotees spend this night in prayer, seeking forgiveness and blessings. Another important practice during Ramadan is giving Zakat al-Fitr, a form of charity given to the poor before the Eid al-Fitr prayer. This offering is obligatory for every Muslim who possesses the minimum amount of wealth necessary to provide for themselves and their family, ensuring the wellbeing of the community's needy during the festive period.

Physical and Spiritual Benefits of Fasting:

The act of fasting allows the body to detoxify and rejuvenate, providing a break for the digestive system and aiding in the removal of toxins from the body. This purification process can lead to improved overall health, including enhanced metabolism and potential weight management benefits. Additionally, the self-discipline and control required during fasting can contribute to increased mental clarity and concentration.

From a spiritual perspective, Ramadan fosters a sense of empathy and compassion for those less fortunate by experiencing hunger firsthand. This empathy can lead to a deeper appreciation for blessings and a heightened sense of gratitude. Furthermore, the practice of self-restraint strengthens one's willpower and resilience, fostering personal growth and character development.

Moreover, fasting encourages introspection and self-reflection, allowing individuals to engage in a deeper spiritual connection with their inner selves and with the divine. It provides an opportunity for believers to cleanse their hearts and minds, seeking forgiveness and spiritual renewal during this sacred time. The heightened focus on spirituality and mindfulness throughout the month of Ramadan cultivates a sense of tranquility and inner peace, nourishing the soul in ways.

In addition to these spiritual and physical benefits, scientific studies have shown that intermittent fasting, such as the practice observed during Ramadan, may have potential health advantages, including improved insulin sensitivity, reduced inflammation, and decreased risk factors for chronic diseases such as diabetes and heart disease. Research suggests that fasting can trigger cellular repair processes and promote longevity, contributing to overall well-being.

Exemptions and Flexibility In Observance:

Fasting during Ramadan is considered a fundamental pillar of Islam, but it is important to acknowledge that there are exemptions and allowances within the practice for those who may face challenges due to health concerns, pregnancy, menstruation, travel, or other valid reasons. These exemptions are not meant to diminish the significance of fasting, but rather to accommodate individuals who may find it difficult or detrimental to their well-being. The Quran explicitly states, 'But if any of you is ill or on a journey, the same number should be made up from other days' (Surah Al-Baqarah 2:184), highlighting the flexibility and understanding inherent in Islamic teachings. Understanding and compassion are integral aspects of religious observance, and these exemptions serve as a means of ensuring that the spiritual benefits of fasting do not outweigh the well-being of the individual. Additionally, exemptions also extend to individuals who are elderly, young children who have not reached the age of puberty, and those who are mentally or physically incapable of fasting. It is crucial for the community and fellow practitioners to recognize and support those who are exempted from fasting, fostering an environment of compassion and inclusivity. Moreover, the concept of fidya, which allows individuals unable to fast to provide meals or sustenance to those in need, exemplifies the compassionate nature of religious observance. This provision not only ensures that the underprivileged receive necessary support but also reinforces the principle of social responsibility within the broader context of Ramadan.

Community and Congregational Aspects:

The month of Ramadan is not only an individual purification process but also a time for strengthening community bonds and fostering a sense of unity among Muslims. Community and congregational aspects play a significant role in enhancing the spiritual experience and social cohesion during this sacred month. The collective observance of fasting, nightly Taraweeh prayers, and communal iftars (breaking of the fast) all serve to highlight the importance of shared religious activities.

One of the most iconic aspects of Ramadan is the special nightly congregational prayers called Taraweeh, performed in mosques or community centers. These extended prayers offer an opportunity for believers to come together and engage in prolonged worship, reciting and reflecting upon the Quran as a unified group. This practice not only deepens individual spirituality but also strengthens the sense of communal devotion to God.

Additionally, the widespread tradition of communal iftars exemplifies the spirit of generosity and hospitality that characterizes Ramadan. Muslims often gather to break their fasts together, whether in local mosques, Islamic centers, or homes. Such communal iftars foster a sense of solidarity and empathy, reminding individuals of the importance of sharing blessings and supporting one another in times of need.

Moreover, the act of giving charity, known as Zakat al-Fitr, further underscores the communal aspects of Ramadan. Muslims are encouraged to donate to those in need before the celebration of Eid al-Fitr, ensuring that everyone can partake in the festivity and joy of the holiday. This charitable practice reinforces the communal responsibility to care for the less fortunate and contributes to the overall sense of unity within the Muslim community.

Beyond these specific practices, the collective experience of fasting itself creates a bond among members of the community. Sharing in the daily discipline of abstaining from food and drink from dawn to sunset fosters empathy and compassion for others' struggles and reinforces the communal commitment to faith and self-improvement.

Eid al-Fitr Celebrations:

Eid al-Fitr, or the "Festival of Breaking the Fast," is a joyous and significant religious holiday celebrated by Muslims worldwide to mark the end of Ramadan, the holy month of fasting. The festive occasion holds immense cultural and spiritual importance, signifying gratitude, unity, and charity. As the crescent moon is sighted, heralding the conclusion of Ramadan, the Muslim community begins preparations for the grandeur of Eid al-Fitr.

The morning of Eid starts with special congregational prayers held in mosques or open prayer grounds. These collective prayers foster a sense of communal harmony and spiritual rejuvenation as individuals and families come together to offer supplications and blessings for all. The traditional Takbir, the glorification of God, resounds through the air, filling hearts with a deep sense of devotion. After the prayers, Muslims greet each other with warm embraces and exchange heartfelt Eid greetings, promoting an atmosphere of love and camaraderie.

Central to the festivities is the act of giving Zakat al-Fitr, a form of charity intended to purify those who fast from any indecent act during the month of Ramadan and provide for the less fortunate. This obligatory almsgiving aims to ensure that everyone can partake in the joyous celebrations of Eid. By doing so, it fosters empathy, compassion, and social solidarity, reinforcing the principles of equality and care within the community.

Culinary delights are another hallmark of Eid al-Fitr. Families prepare sumptuous feasts comprising traditional dishes and sweets, representing the abundance and blessings bestowed upon them. Sharing meals with family, friends, and neighbors symbolizes hospitality, generosity, and familial bonds, setting the stage for convivial gatherings and shared warmth.

Moreover, the custom of exchanging gifts during Eid al-Fitr further strengthens personal relationships and conveys appreciation and affection. The act of giving gifts reflects gratitude for the blessings received and embodies the Islamic value of reciprocity while deepening connections among family members, colleagues, and friends.

Furthermore, dressing in new attire for Eid conveys reverence for the occasion and serves as a mark of spiritual renewal and self-purification. People adorn themselves in their finest clothing, often purchased or gifted for this special day, signifying purity of heart and the desire to present oneself in the best manner before God.

The celebration of Eid al-Fitr extends beyond individual homes to embrace the wider community, where charitable events, fairs, and entertainment activities cater to people of all ages. These inclusive festivities promote social cohesion, strengthen communal ties, and create lasting memories for children and adults alike.

Chapter XIII
PRAYERS AND GLORIFICATIONS

Significance of Prayer in Daily Life:

Prayer holds significance in the daily life of a believer, serving as a spiritual anchor amidst the tumultuous seas of worldly affairs. It is a divine connection to the Creator, an opportunity for reflection, and a source of solace in challenging times. The act of prayer transcends mere physical movements and recitations; it represents submission, gratitude, and humility before the Almighty. Through prayer, individuals harness a sense of purpose and mindfulness that enriches their daily experiences, fostering a deeper spiritual awareness and resilience in the face of adversity. Moreover, prayer aids in maintaining a balanced perspective, by reminding believers to prioritize their spiritual well-being alongside their material pursuits, fostering a harmonious and holistic approach to life. In essence, prayer imbues everyday routines with spiritual significance, transforming mundane actions into acts of worship and devotion. Furthermore, the discipline of regular prayer cultivates a sense of discipline, punctuality, and consistency, instilling these virtues into the fabric of daily life. By acknowledging the significance of prayer in daily life, individuals can aspire to integrate spirituality into all facets of their existence, ensuring that every thought, action, and interaction aligns with the values and teachings espoused in the Quran. This realization fosters a deep sense of inner peace and fulfillment, enabling believers to front on to life's complexities with fortitude. As such, the significance of prayer in daily life becomes a transformative force, shaping attitudes, behaviors, and relationships.

The Five Daily Prayers:

The five daily prayers, known as Salat, serve as a connection to the Divine. The timing and structure of these prayers are not only integral to the practice of Islam but also embody moments of spiritual devotion and grounding throughout the day. With roots tracing back to the Prophet Muhammad's night journey and ascension to the heavens, the establishment of the five daily prayers became obligatory for every adult Muslim as a means of maintaining a constant awareness of God. Each prayer, from Fajr (pre-dawn) to Isha (nightfall), has its specific timing and unique set of units, or Rak'ahs, reinforcing the significance of regular spiritual engagement. The rhythmic call to prayer, or Adhan, echoing through the atmosphere, marks the commencement of each Salat, acting as a reminder to pause from worldly affairs and turn towards the divine presence. Fajr, the dawn prayer, aligns with the beginning of a new day, invoking a sense of renewal and seeking blessings as the world awakens. Dhuhr, the midday prayer, serves as a brief interlude from daily activities, fostering a moment for reflection and contemplation amid the hustle of life. Asr, the afternoon prayer, calls upon the faithful to halt their obligations and refocus on faith during the latter part of the day, while Maghrib, the evening prayer, coincides with the spectacular setting of the sun, symbolizing gratitude for sustenance and nourishment. Lastly, Isha, the night prayer, encourages self-examination and introspection before retiring for the night, unwinding the mind amidst the tranquility of darkness. The meticulous timing and order of these prayers exemplify the cyclical nature of human existence, providing individuals with the opportunity to engage with their spirituality at various points within the daily rhythm.

Importance of Khushu:

Khushu, or concentration in prayer, represents a state of humility, reverence, and complete mindfulness during the act of worship. The Quran emphasizes the importance of khushu in numerous verses, urging believers to establish their prayers with earnest devotion and focus. Achieving khushu requires inner tranquility, heartfelt sincerity, and undivided attention to the words recited and actions performed during salah.

In the bustling rhythm of modern life, maintaining khushu can be challenging. Distractions from the external world, racing thoughts, and wavering emotions often threaten to disrupt one's presence of mind during prayer. However, recognizing the value of khushu empowers individuals to actively cultivate this essential aspect of their spiritual practice.

The Prophet Muhammad (peace be upon him) exemplified remarkable khushu in his prayers, demonstrating the depth of his connection with the Almighty. He would pray with such utmost concentration that his movements and supplications resonated with sincerity. His teachings emphasize the need for believers to guard against heedlessness and strive to attain khushu, as it elevates the worshipper's connection to Allah and purifies the soul.

Attaining khushu extends beyond the physical aspects of prayer; it encompasses the purification of the heart and the aspiration to attain spiritual closeness to God. The prayer should serve as a moment of introspection, where one humbly acknowledges their own limitations and seeks the blessings and guidance of the Divine. By nurturing khushu, individuals strengthen their relationship with their Creator and embody submission, awe, and gratitude in their worship.

Various practices can aid in fostering khushu, including finding a tranquil environment for prayer, reciting the Quran with contemplation, and reflecting on the meanings of the invocations uttered. Additionally, dedicating time to seek forgiveness, offer gratitude, and invoke blessings upon the Prophet further enriches the experience of prayer with khushu.

Glorifications - Tasbih, Tahmid, and Takbir:

Glorifying and praising the Almighty is an integral part of Islamic daily devotion. The acts of Tasbih, Tahmid, and Takbir manifest one's gratitude, reverence, and submission to the divine. Through these forms of glorification, believers express their deep connection with Allah and find solace in His remembrance.

Tasbih, often performed using prayer beads, involves the repetitive recitation of phrases such as 'SubhanAllah' (Glory be to Allah), 'Alhamdulillah' (Praise be to Allah), and 'Allahu Akbar' (Allah is the Greatest). This practice aids in centering the mind and heart on the magnificence of the Creator, fostering inner peace and spiritual awareness.

Tahmid, the act of praising Allah, encapsulates the essence of acknowledging His boundless mercy, abundant blessings, and unwavering support. By uttering phrases like 'Alhamdulillah' and expressing gratitude for all that has been bestowed upon them, individuals reaffirm their reliance on the divine and recognize their position as humble servants.

Similarly, Takbir involves proclaiming the greatness of Allah, affirming His supreme authority and eminence. Through phrases such as 'Allahu Akbar' and 'La ilaha illallah' (There is no god but Allah), believers declare their unwavering faith and reinforce their commitment to the principles of monotheism.

Integrating these glorifications into daily prayers and moments of reflection elevates the spiritual experience, fostering a deeper sense of connection and adoration for the divine. It allows individuals to transcend the mundane and connect with the transcendent, infusing their lives with purpose, humility, and mindfulness.

Furthermore, incorporating these glorifications into daily routines serves as a powerful reminder of the omnipresence of the divine, infusing each moment with a heightened awareness of God's omnipotence and benevolence. By engaging in Tasbih, Tahmid, and Takbir, individuals cultivate a state of constant remembrance and acknowledgment, resulting in a transformation of their inner spiritual landscape.

Du'as - Personal Supplications post-Prayer:

Du'as, or personal supplications, offer a direct channel for communication with the Divine, allowing individuals to express their gratitude, seek guidance, and request blessings from Allah. Post-prayer du'as serve as moments of intimate connection with the Creator, offering an opportunity for reflection, humility, and earnest entreaty.

Following the completion of the formal prayer, engaging in du'as allows individuals to extend their spiritual engagement beyond the ritualistic actions. It's a time for personal introspection and heartfelt dialogue with the Almighty. These supplications can range from seeking forgiveness for one's shortcomings to asking for strength in facing life's challenges.

Additionally, du'as provide a platform for believers to express gratitude for the countless blessings they receive daily. This expression of thanks fosters a sense of contentment and ultimately strengthens one's faith and connection to Allah. One of the most beautiful aspects of du'as is their ability to encompass the entire spectrum of human emotions, serving as a form of solace during times of distress and a medium for expressing joy and gratitude in times of prosperity.

Furthermore, the act of making du'as post-prayer serves as a demonstration of submission and reliance on Allah's infinite mercy and wisdom. This practice reinforces the understanding that all outcomes are ultimately in His hands, fostering a sense of acceptance and trust in His divine plan.

It is important for individuals to recognize that there are no specific prescribed formulae for personal supplications; one may speak to Allah in any language and at any time, expressing their innermost thoughts and desires. This accessibility underscores the inclusive nature of Islam and showcases the personal and direct relationship each believer has with Allah. This concept also emphasizes the compassion and understanding that Allah extends to His creation.

Role of the Mosque in Community Prayer:

Within the context of daily devotions, mosques play a crucial role in facilitating community prayer, offering an environment conducive to spiritual reflection and unity among believers. The physical architecture of mosques, often adorned with designs and calligraphy, serves as a visual reminder of the divine presence, inspiring reverence and humility in those who enter.

Community prayer at the mosque provides an opportunity for mutual support and solidarity among worshippers. It fosters a sense of belonging and shared commitment to upholding religious traditions. Through congregational prayers, individuals from diverse backgrounds come together, transcending social barriers and connecting on a deeper spiritual level. This collective experience reinforces the notion of Islam as a unifying force, emphasizing the importance of harmony and cooperation within the community.

Furthermore, the mosque serves as a center for spiritual education and guidance, offering resources for learning about the principles and practices of prayer. Imams and knowledgeable community leaders may deliver sermons and workshops focused on enhancing the quality of prayer and cultivating a sincere connection with the Divine. These educational initiatives aim to instill an understanding of the significance of prayer in the lives of believers, motivating them to engage in daily devotions with mindfulness and devotion.

In addition to the spiritual benefits, the mosque promotes social cohesion and charitable activities within the community. By coming together for congregational prayers, individuals also engage in acts of charity, support initiatives for the less fortunate, and address the needs of the community as a whole. This emphasis on communal welfare demonstrates the broader societal impact of the mosque as a hub for promoting compassion, empathy, and altruism among its members.

Praying with Intent - Achieving Spiritual Closeness:

Achieving spiritual closeness through prayer requires a deep understanding of the intention behind each act of worship. The sincerity of one's intention is paramount in creating a connection with the divine. When approaching prayers, it is essential to focus on the purpose of the prayer, seeking to attain nearness to Allah and humbly submitting to His guidance and wisdom. Intention shapes the entire experience of prayer, infusing it with meaning and significance. As the Quran emphasizes, 'And they were not commanded except to worship Allah, [being] sincere to Him in religion' (Quran 98:5). Thus, praying with intent means wholeheartedly devoting oneself to the worship of the Creator.

To achieve spiritual closeness during prayers, one should strive to eliminate distractions and foster a reverent atmosphere. This involves preparing both mentally and physically before engaging in prayer. Finding a peaceful and clean space, freeing the mind from worldly concerns, and assuming a posture of humility are essential steps in aligning one's focus toward the divine. Furthermore, purifying the heart from negative emotions and distractions can significantly enhance one's ability to connect spiritually during prayer. Cultivating an attitude of gratitude and mindfulness can bring about a state of spiritual clarity that is conducive to achieving a closeness to Allah.

Moreover, understanding the meanings of the supplications and verses recited during prayer can deepen the spiritual experience. Reflecting on the words being recited, whether during prostration, bowing, or standing, can amplify the spiritual impact of the prayer. Internalizing the messages and seeking to implement their teachings in daily life can lead to a heightened sense of spiritual enlightenment.

Additionally, fostering a consistent prayer routine contributes to developing a spiritual connection. Regular, timely prayers create a rhythm that permeates one's daily life with devotion and humility. It is through this ongoing dedication that the heart becomes attuned to the remembrance of Allah, thus achieving spiritual closeness with each prostration and utterance of glorification. These inward moments of connection during prayer form the foundation for overarching spiritual awareness and tranquility in all aspects of life.

Chapter XIV
THE PURPOSE OF LIFE

The Road to Righteousness:

Life is a web of experiences and challenges, designed to test our moral fiber and spiritual resolve. In the Quran, it is repeatedly emphasized that these tests are necessary for the growth and purification of the human soul. Divine testing serves as a means to differentiate between those who stand steadfast in their faith and those who falter in the face of adversity. It is through these trials that individuals have the opportunity to showcase their commitment to righteousness and obedience to God.

The concept of divine testing can be traced back to the stories of the prophets and righteous individuals mentioned in the scriptures. Their lives serve as powerful examples of how they endured immense trials and tribulations with unwavering faith, ultimately earning God's favor and blessings. Their stories demonstrate that every hardship, setback, and difficulty is a potential opportunity for personal and spiritual growth.

Furthermore, divine testing is not solely a mechanism for individual evaluation, but also a means for establishing justice and equity in the world. It serves as a reminder that the ultimate judgment belongs to the Divine, and that every action and intention will be accounted for accordingly. This understanding encourages believers to maintain integrity and righteousness in all aspects of life, knowing that their actions are being observed and will eventually be weighed against their deeds.

In facing righteousness, it is essential to approach divine testing with patience, perseverance, and unwavering trust in the wisdom and mercy of the Divine. Each challenge presents an opportunity to strengthen one's character, deepen one's faith, and purify one's soul. Understanding that these tests are part of a greater divine plan can offer solace and fortitude during times of hardship.

Ultimately, divine testing serves as a means of refining and elevating the human spirit, providing opportunities for introspection, repentance, and self-improvement. It reinforces the belief that trials and tribulations with patience and gratitude can lead to a state of spiritual elevation and closeness to the Divine.

Trials and Tribulations:

Life is a journey filled with trials and tribulations that test the human spirit. From the earliest scriptures to modern experiences, the narrative of human existence has been rich with stories of perseverance in the face of adversity. The concept of trials and tribulations is deeply rooted in the wisdom of the Quran, where believers are reminded that challenges are an inherent part of the human experience. It is through these trials that individuals are tested, their faith strengthened, and their character refined. The tales of prophets facing immense hardships, only to emerge with steadfast faith and resilience, offer insights into the human condition. Whether it is the story of Prophet Job immense suffering, or Prophet Moses leading his people through countless trials in the wilderness, the Quran showcases how facing tribulations can lead to spiritual growth and transformation. Moreover, the experiences of renowned figures from history serve as poignant reminders of the resilience and fortitude required to overcome life's hurdles. Through the lens of these historical insights, individuals can gain a deeper understanding of the universal nature of trials and tribulations. This perspective can provide solace during times of personal difficulty and serve as a source of inspiration for rising above challenges. Furthermore, the examination of the human experience in relation to trials and tribulations sheds light on the redemptive power of faith and resilience. In facing trials, individuals are called upon to embody virtues such as patience, gratitude, and perseverance. These invaluable traits not only enable individuals to weather the storms of life but also empower them to emerge stronger and more compassionate. The concept of trials and tribulations extends beyond personal hardships and encompasses the larger societal and global challenges faced by humanity. From wars to natural disasters, the collective human experience has borne witness to innumerable trials that have tested the resilience of entire communities.

Faith in Action:

Living righteously is an active, deliberate pursuit of virtuous conduct in every aspect of life. Our faith inspires us to embody compassion, justice, and moral integrity in all our interactions, both with fellow human beings and with the world around us. This proactive stance demands that we constantly evaluate our intentions and actions, striving for consistency between our beliefs and our behavior. It requires us to be conscientious stewards of the blessings entrusted to us, acknowledging that our choices and deeds hold consequences not only in this world but in the divine realm as well. Thus, faith in action calls for an unwavering commitment to upholding righteousness, even in the face of adversity.

When we integrate faith into our daily lives, we become agents of positive change, influencing those around us through our exemplary conduct and sincere dedication to ethical principles. Fostering harmony and empathy, we contribute to the greater good of society, seeking to uplift and support our fellow human beings in their individual journeys toward righteousness. Moreover, living righteously means adhering to the core values espoused by our faith, such as integrity, honesty, kindness, and respect for all creation. We recognize that our actions reflect our beliefs and serve as a testament to our commitment to lead a purposeful life attuned to divine guidance.

Furthermore, embodying faith through righteous living enables us to front on to complex moral dilemmas with wisdom and prudence. It empowers us to make decisions that are deeply rooted in our spiritual convictions, fostering an inner strength that fortifies our resolve in times of moral challenge. By aligning our intentions with divine will, we anchor ourselves in principles that transcend the transient allure of worldly temptations, thereby remaining steadfast on the path of righteousness. Through our actions, we demonstrate to others the transformative power of faith, inspiring them to embrace their own spiritual journeys with renewed fervor and clarity.

Role of Intention:

The intention, or niyyah, serves as the driving force behind our actions and endeavors, imbuing them with spiritual significance and moral weight. As stated in a hadith of the Prophet Muhammad, 'Actions are but by intention, and every man shall have only that which he intended.' This statement underscores the inherent value and emphasis placed on the purity and sincerity of one's intentions.

Aligning with divine will necessitates adopting pure and noble intentions in all aspects of life. The intention acts as the compass guiding our thoughts, words, and deeds towards righteousness and goodness. It is a conscientious choice to align our innermost motivations with the ethical teachings and guidance provided within the Quran and Sunnah. By acknowledging the importance of intention, individuals strive to mold their actions into acts of worship and service to humanity, thus fulfilling their ultimate purpose in this world.

Moreover, intention serves as a filter through which the quality and acceptability of our deeds are evaluated. The Quran teaches that the acceptance and reward for any action is contingent upon the purity of its intention. Hence, the role of intention extends beyond mere motivation and encompasses the assurance of spiritual integrity and alignment with divine pleasure.

The practice of aligning intention with divine will instills a heightened awareness of consequences and accountability. It encourages introspection and self-reflection, prompting individuals to evaluate the righteousness and justification of their goals and pursuits. This mindfulness fosters a sense of responsibility and volition, enabling individuals to consciously experience their lives in accordance with the ethical standards set forth by Islam.

By aligning with divine will through sincere intention, individuals transit from performing mundane tasks to executing acts of worship and spiritual devotion. Simple daily routines, when infused with righteous intentions, become potent sources of reward and spiritual fulfillment. Whether it is charity, family responsibilities, or professional conduct, the act of aligning intentions with divine will elevates these endeavors to the status of virtuous conduct and an expression of faith.

Mercy and Compassion:

God's mercy is often portrayed as an all-encompassing attribute that transcends human understanding. It is through this divine mercy that believers find solace and rejuvenation in times of distress and hardship, as it serves as a testament to the unconditional love and forgiveness offered by the

Almighty. The Quran repeatedly emphasizes the boundless mercy of God, stating that His mercy encompasses all things. This realization shapes the believer's outlook, instilling a sense of hope, gratitude, and humility as they experience life's myriad challenges.

Compassion, on the other hand, manifests as a call for believers to extend kindness and empathy toward others, thereby mirroring the merciful attributes of the divine. The Prophet Muhammad, peace be upon him, was a paragon of compassion, exhibiting unwavering kindness and benevolence even towards those who opposed him. His actions serve as an example for believers to embody compassion in their interactions with others. Cultivating a compassionate heart enables individuals to not only receive God's grace but also become conduits of divine mercy in their communities. This reciprocity of mercy enriches the believer's spiritual journey, fostering inner peace and harmony.

As followers seek to align themselves with the divine will, embracing and radiating mercy becomes a fundamental component of their spiritual growth. The Quran further expounds the correlation between showing mercy and receiving mercy from the Creator, highlighting that those who show mercy will be shown mercy by the Most Merciful. Consequently, it becomes incumbent upon believers to cultivate a disposition of compassion and forgiveness, recognizing that these qualities pave the way for experiencing the boundless grace of the divine. This evokes a deep sense of responsibility and accountability, urging believers to integrate acts of mercy and compassion into their daily lives. By making sincere efforts to embody these virtues, believers open their hearts to the bountiful mercy and grace bestowed by God, ultimately finding solace and tranquility amidst the trials and triumphs of life.

Chapter XV
WORLDLY PLEASURES

The Consequences of Excess:

Excessive pursuit of worldly pleasures can have impacts on the soul, often leading to a sense of emptiness and spiritual disconnection. When individuals prioritize material possessions, hedonistic pursuits, or selfish desires above all else, they risk losing sight of their higher purpose and spiritual well-being. The Quran provides insightful guidance on the consequences of such excess, cautioning against the potential harm it can inflict on the soul. By delving into this topic, we gain a deeper understanding of the balance between worldly indulgence and spiritual fulfillment.

The ramifications of excessive attachment to worldly pleasures manifest in various forms. One of the most evident impacts is the erosion of inner peace and contentment. When individuals become consumed by the pursuit of transient pleasures, they often experience a perpetual sense of restlessness and dissatisfaction. This insatiable quest for immediate gratification can lead to an emotional void, creating a barrier to experiencing genuine joy and inner tranquility. Moreover, excessive indulgence can engender feelings of guilt, shame, and moral conflict, further diminishing the soul's vitality.

Furthermore, the undue emphasis on worldly pleasures can overshadow one's spiritual growth and development. This preoccupation with materialism and superficial gratification detracts from the pursuit of higher virtues and ethical conduct. It hampers introspection and self-improvement, inhibiting the individual from cultivating qualities such as compassion, generosity, and humility. As a result, the soul may become ensnared in a cycle of self-serving behaviors and attitudes, hindering its progress towards spiritual enlightenment and moral refinement.

In addition to personal implications, the consequences of excess extend to interpersonal relationships and societal dynamics. The insidious allure of wealth, status, and instant gratification can foster an environment of competition, envy, and divisive social hierarchies. This intrudes upon the harmonious coexistence and mutual support that are fundamental to a cohesive community. Moreover, unchecked pursuit of worldly pleasures can overshadow empathy and compassion, leading to a lack of concern for the welfare of others and a decline in communal bonds.

Acknowledging the gravity of these consequences prompts an imperative shift towards cultivating moderation and self-restraint. Embracing the Islamic perspective on moderation highlights the importance of temperance and mindfulness in facing the transient nature of worldly pleasures. By adopting a balanced approach, individuals can safeguard their souls from the detrimental effects of excess, fostering sustainable fulfillment and spiritual harmony.

Treading the Path of Moderation:

In Islamic teachings, the concept of moderation is deeply rooted in guiding individuals towards a balanced and purposeful life. The Quran and the Hadith emphasize the importance of avoiding extremes and adopting a middle way in all aspects of existence. This principle applies not only to matters of material possessions and wealth but also to emotions, relationships, and spirituality. By treading the path of moderation, individuals can attain harmony within themselves and their interactions with others.

Islamic perspectives on moderation advocate for the avoidance of excess and deficiency in lifestyle choices. The Prophet Muhammad (peace be upon him) exemplified this through his simple and modest living, demonstrating that richness of character and faith transcends material opulence. From dietary habits to financial conduct, Muslims are encouraged to maintain equilibrium, reflecting gratitude and contentment in both abundance and scarcity.

Beyond tangible possessions, moderation extends to the realm of emotions and behaviors. Islam emphasizes self-restraint and composure, urging believers to front on to desires and impulses with mindfulness and conscientiousness. By doing so, one can cultivate inner peace and resilience, fostering a tranquil state of mind amidst life's challenges and triumphs.

Spirituality also forms a cornerstone of Islamic moderation. Through regular acts of worship and connection with the Divine, individuals can deepen their sense of purpose and transcend fleeting temptations. Islamic teachings underscore the pursuit of spiritual fulfillment over fleeting gratification, encouraging adherence to moral values and virtuous conduct.

Furthermore, the concept of moderateness is pivotal in fostering harmonious relationships within society. By respecting diverse perspectives and avoiding extremism, individuals contribute to societal cohesion and unity. Mutual understanding and tolerance serve as fundamental tenets in promoting peaceful coexistence and collaborative progress.

Eternal Rewards:

The pursuit of eternal rewards through prioritizing spiritual goals is a fundamental aspect of the Islamic faith. Through the teachings of Islam, we are guided to seek balance between our worldly responsibilities and our spiritual aspirations. The

Quran emphasizes the importance of striving for righteousness and the prioritization of fulfilling our spiritual duties. By focusing on humility, empathy, and generosity, we pave the way for reaping eternal rewards in the afterlife.

Prioritizing spiritual goals entails aligning our intentions and actions with the divine principles advocated in Islamic teachings. It involves nurturing a deep sense of gratitude, compassion, and selflessness in our interactions with others. By emphasizing the significance of spiritual growth and moral conduct, we strive to strengthen our connection with the Creator and contribute positively to the world around us.

Furthermore, the concept of eternal rewards serves as a reminder of the transient nature of worldly possessions and pleasures. Rather than being consumed by material pursuits and temporary gratification, believers are encouraged to invest their energies in acts of worship, charity, and kindness. By dedicating ourselves to self-improvement and serving the community, we embody the values of integrity and benevolence that lead to lasting spiritual fulfillment.

In pursuing spiritual goals, we embrace the notion of accountability and seek to attain closeness to Allah. This requires a steadfast commitment to fulfilling obligations towards prayer, charity, and the pursuit of knowledge. By internalizing the significance of these spiritual practices, we fortify our resilience against the distractions and temptations of the world, anchoring ourselves in the pursuit of eternal rewards.

Ultimately, prioritizing spiritual goals shapes our perspective, motivations, and actions, guiding us towards a life of purpose and fulfillment. Through this dedication, we lay the foundation for rewards in the Hereafter, fostering a sense of hope, perseverance, and steadfastness in the face of life's trials and tribulations.

Chapter XVI
DIVINE VIGILANCE, RESTLESSNESS, AND THRONE

The concept of divine vigilance is derived from the belief in an omnipotent and omniscient deity who actively maintains and sustains the world. In Islam, the idea of divine vigilance, known as 'Rahman' and 'Rahim', emphasizes God's constant mercy and compassion towards his creation. This perspective underscores the inherent benevolence and active involvement of the divine in human affairs.

The Quran describes the throne of God, known as the 'Arsh,' as a symbol of His sovereignty and omnipotence. The Islamic tradition emphasizes the exalted nature of God's throne, portraying it as a manifestation of His supreme authority and dominion over all creation. Furthermore, Islamic theology emphasizes the divine attributes of mercy and justice in relation to the concept of God's rule, fostering an understanding of balance and harmony within His governance.

From an allegorical perspective, the throne embodies the heightened celestial authority of God, signifying His supreme rulership over all creation. It encapsulates the divine majesty and unassailable power that governs the universe. Furthermore, the throne symbolizes the immutable cosmic order and stability inherent in God's reign, offering reassurance to believers and reinforcing their faith in His unwavering control of existence. On a more literal plane, the throne represents the tangible manifestation of divine authority, serving as a physical locus of governance in the celestial realm. This tangible embodiment asserts God's omnipresence and eternal vigilance, establishing a resonant connection between the heavens and the earthly domain.

Regarding God's Restlessness, it represents the perpetual movement and activity of God in sustaining and governing the universe. This divine restlessness is far from being characterized by agitation or anxiety; rather, it embodies an unceasing state of active engagement and vigilant oversight over all creation. The Quranic and prophetic traditions expound on this concept, affirming that God's restlessness is synonymous with His tireless care, protection, and direction of the cosmos.

Continuous creation serves as a tangible manifestation of God's eternal restlessness. It signifies His ongoing act of bringing forth existence and maintaining the balance and harmony within the cosmic order. From the graceful dance of celestial bodies to the interplay of ecosystems on Earth, the divine restlessness unfurls in every phenomenon, signaling a ceaseless outpouring of creative energy and sustaining mercy.

Moreover, guardianship emerges as an inseparable facet of God's restlessness. It epitomizes His unwavering commitment to nurture, guide, and support His creatures throughout their existential journey. The bountiful provisions of sustenance, the guidance imparted through revelations, and the solace found in times of tribulation all bear witness to the encompassing embrace of divine guardianship. This divine attribute furnishes humanity with a sense of security and belonging, assuring them that they are never bereft of God's benevolent watchfulness.

On the other hand, God's essence is not limited by any spatial or temporal boundaries. This transcendence extends beyond human comprehension and defies conventional notions of existence. The omnipresence of God represents an absolute, ineffable reality that transcends the mortal realm. It is a concept that has stirred philosophical inquiry and provided spiritual solace to believers across diverse traditions.

Chapter XVII
THE UNSHARED AUTHORITY OF THE CREATOR

The Holy Quran portraits God as the eternal and unchanging reality that transcends the temporal realm. Scriptural narratives and exhortations affirm the intrinsic independence of God, showcasing His immeasurable grace and authority as the sole source of guidance and wisdom. These scriptural evidences and references provide a compelling basis for believers to contemplate and internalize the significance of God's absolute independence within their spiritual journey. Numerous verses explicitly emphasize the self-sufficiency and sovereignty of God. For instance, Surah Al-Ikhlas (112:1-4) succinctly encapsulates the idea of God's absolute independence, stating that He neither begets nor is begotten, and there is none comparable unto Him. This underlines the Quranic portrayal of God as free from any form of dependence or neediness, highlighting His unmatched perfection and omnipotence.

In delving into the theological underpinnings of divine sovereignty, we encounter the fundamental attributes of omnipotence and omniscience that define the nature of God's rule. Omnipotence, indicating God's all-encompassing power, suggests an authority that transcends human comprehension. It is the basis for the belief in God's ability to enact His will and to maintain absolute control over the universe. This omnipotence embodies not just physical strength, but also moral authority, displaying the divine capacity to govern with justice and wisdom beyond the limitations of mortal understanding.

Conversely, omniscience reflects the comprehensive knowledge possessed by the Creator, encompassing all events, both past and future, along with the deepest thoughts and intentions of every being. This attribute reinforces the concept of divine sovereignty, as it signifies that no aspect of creation exists outside the purview of God's awareness. The combination of omnipotence and omniscience offers a foundation for understanding the unshared authority of the Creator, as it delineates a form of governance that is not contingent on any external factors or limitations.

Moreover, the theological significance of these attributes extends beyond mere conceptual understanding. They serve as pillars supporting the faith and devotion of believers, fostering an unwavering trust in the supremacy of God's rule amidst the complexities and trials of existence. The belief in God's omnipotence and omniscience engenders a sense of security and dependence on the divine will, shaping individual conduct and societal ethos through the assurance that all actions occur within the framework of an overarching, purposeful design. On the other hand, while humanity is endowed with agency, the omnipotence and omniscience of God imply an interplay between human volition and the ultimate plan of the Creator.

On the other hand, philosophers and theologians have long grappled with the concept of God's unshared rule, delving into inquiries that seek to unveil divine sovereignty. One prevailing philosophical perspective examines the implications of an all-encompassing, unchallenged authority governing the cosmos. It presents a compelling argument for the coexistence of human free will within the framework of God's ultimate supremacy. This contemplation asserts that while humans possess the capacity for independent thought and action, the course of their lives intersects with the divine providence ordained by the Creator's unshared rule. Through this lens, human agency harmonizes with the immutable decree of the Almighty, reinforcing the notion of a predetermined cosmic design guided by divine wisdom. Furthermore, philosophical discourse often explores the significance of moral responsibility in the context of God's unchallenged authority.

The ethical implications of acknowledging the absolute sovereignty of the Creator prompt reflections on the nature of virtue, accountability, and the inherent moral fabric woven into the human experience. Philosophers seek to elucidate the relationship between divine governance and human morality, discerning the interplay of conscience and complacency within the framework of God's unshared rule. Additionally, philosophical perspectives on God's unchallenged authority may also delve into suffering, justice, and theodicy. Contemplations on these themes endeavor to reconcile the existence of adversity and inequity with the belief in an omnipotent and benevolent Creator. By examining the interconnectedness of human tribulations and divine providence, philosophers endeavor to unravel the enigmatic facets of God's unshared rule in the face of worldly afflictions and moral dilemmas.

Regarding the concept of divine law, it is inexorably linked to the cosmic order, serving as the framework through which the universe operates in alignment with the will of the Creator. Divine law is a testament to the unwavering sovereignty of God, entailing the fundamental principles by which all creation abides. This transcendent law encompasses not only moral and ethical directives for humanity but also governs the natural world, celestial bodies, and the balance inherent in the cosmos. As such, it is incumbent upon individuals to recognize and adhere to these laws, fostering harmony and equilibrium within the wider fabric of existence.

The establishment of divine law serves as a compelling demonstration of the Creator's unassailable jurisdiction over all realms, instilling reverence and awe in those who contemplate its implications. Through divine law, the interconnectedness of all facets of creation becomes apparent, underscoring the sublime wisdom that governs the universe. It beckons individuals to reflect on their roles as custodians entrusted with upholding the integrity of this divine mandate, thereby contributing to the preservation of order and coherence within the cosmic tapestry.

In addition, divine law offers a robust foundation for ethical conduct, guiding human endeavors towards righteousness, justice, and compassion. Its resonance extends beyond mere compliance, urging individuals to embrace a conscientious and principled way of life that mirrors the transcendent virtues embedded within the fabric of creation. Moreover, divine law engenders a sense of responsibility and accountability, emphasizing the imperative of stewardship and custodianship over the earth and its inhabitants. It imparts an understanding of the interconnectedness between the tangible and intangible, accentuating the pervasive influence of divine law in every aspect of human experience.

Contemplation of the cosmic order, underpinned by divine law, invites individuals to recognize the divine orchestration permeating every domain of existence, from the infinitesimal to the infinite. This contemplation evokes an appreciation for the symphony of the cosmos, unveiling the majesty and precision with which every element of the universe coalesces in consonance with divine edicts.

Chapter XVIII
COSMIC ORDER

The Quranic View of the Cosmos:

The Quran presents a comprehensive perspective on the cosmos, offering insights that transcend the limitations of human knowledge and understanding. From the very beginning, the Quran emphasizes the magnificence and orderliness of the universe as a clear sign of divine wisdom and design. The celestial bodies, including the stars, planets, and galaxies, are described as obedient to God's command, moving in their precise orbits according to His will.

Furthermore, the Quran expounds on the purposeful creation of the heavens and the earth, highlighting the harmony and balance inherent in their design. It portrays the cosmos as a manifestation of God's infinite power and creativity, inviting humanity to ponder over the patterns and systems embedded within the celestial realm. The Quranic portrayal of the cosmos serves to remind individuals of their humble place within the grandeur of creation, fostering a sense of awe, reverence, and contemplation.

Moreover, the Quran underscores the transient nature of the material world, contrasting it with the nature of the spiritual realm. It elucidates the temporal cycles of day and night, the changing phases of the moon, and the life-nurturing qualities of the sun, all of which reflect the order and purpose woven into the fabric of the cosmos by the Divine Creator.

Additionally, the Quran contains verses that invite humanity to reflect upon the signs present in the natural world, encouraging them to seek knowledge, explore the mysteries of the universe, and recognize the interconnectedness of all creation.

The Quranic view of the cosmos thus aligns with the pursuit of scientific inquiry, implying a holistic approach to understanding the wonders of the natural world.

Furthermore, the Quran presents the cosmos as a source of spiritual guidance and reflection, urging individuals to look beyond the surface of astronomical phenomena. It prompts believers to contemplate the deeper meanings and symbolism embedded in the celestial bodies, guiding them towards a deeper appreciation of the divine attributes and the metaphysical realities underlying the physical universe.

Scientifical Understanding - Ancient and Modern Insights:

Ancient cultures such as the Babylonians, Egyptians, and Greeks fervently pursued astronomical knowledge, meticulously recording planetary movements and celestial events. Their keen observations laid the groundwork for early astronomical theories and inspired awe-inspiring mythologies that attempted to rationalize the mysteries of heavenly bodies. These legacies demonstrate the pursuit of scientific understanding in diverse cultural contexts.

The transition to the modern era witnessed a monumental leap in humanity's comprehension of the cosmos. Pioneering figures like Copernicus, Galileo, and Kepler revolutionized astronomical thought, challenging long-held beliefs and introducing innovative models of planetary motion and gravitational dynamics. The marriage of empirical observation with mathematical precision paved the way for modern astrophysics, enabling humanity to fathom the vastness and complexity of the universe with unprecedented clarity.

Contemporary cosmic exploration continues to push the boundaries of scientific inquiry, propelled by advancements in space technology and interdisciplinary collaboration. The discovery of exoplanets, black holes, and cosmic microwave background radiation represents remarkable milestones in our quest to unravel the enigmas of the cosmos. Furthermore, ongoing efforts to probe dark matter, dark energy, and cosmic inflation testify to the relentless pursuit of scientific elucidation that characterizes the current epoch.

In recounting this historical trajectory, it becomes evident that the Qur'an, revealed over fourteen centuries ago, anticipates various celestial realities and aligns with some principles elucidated by modern astrophysics. This convergence underscores the prescience of Qur'anic insights regarding natural phenomena, inviting contemporary scholars to explore the compatibility between Islamic scripture and scientific inquiry.

Cosmos, Aesthetic Harmony in Divine Creation:

As we gaze into the night sky, we are presented with a breathtaking tapestry of stars, planets, and galaxies, each playing their part in a dance choreographed by the laws of physics and guided by the hand of divine providence. From the graceful orbits of the planets to the fiery birth and death of stars, the cosmos exudes an elegance that inspires awe and wonder. In exploring the harmonious order of the universe, we begin to unravel the layers of meaning and significance woven into its very fabric. It is within the cosmic ballet that we witness the sublime artistry of the Creator, manifest in the exquisite balance and precision that governs the cosmos.

The aesthetic harmony of the cosmos extends beyond its visual splendor to encompass a deeper resonance with the human spirit. The rhythms of the celestial bodies, from the rhythmic phases of the moon to the annual passage of constellations across the night sky, have served as sources of inspiration for artists, poets, and philosophers throughout history. The patterns and cycles observed in the cosmos reflect a beauty that transcends cultural and temporal boundaries, inviting contemplation and reflection on the nature of existence and the divine origin of creation.

Moreover, the cosmic order bears testimony to a divine intelligence that surpasses human comprehension. The equilibrium of planetary orbits, the gravitational forces that shape the fabric of space-time, and the symmetrical patterns seen in galactic formations all point to an underlying design that speaks of a purposeful intent. It is through the lens of scientific inquiry and spiritual reflection that we begin to discern the interconnectedness of the cosmos and its role in fostering a sense of cosmic interconnectedness.

In contemplating the aesthetic harmony of the cosmos, we are compelled to ponder the relationship between faith and science. While scientific inquiry seeks to unravel the mechanics and laws governing the universe, faith offers a lens through which to perceive the transcendent significance of the cosmic order. The interplay between faith and science serves to enrich our understanding of the cosmos, unveiling layers of meaning that transcend empirical observation alone. Thus, the exploration of the aesthetic harmony in divine creation invites us to embark on a journey of discovery that seeks to bridge the realms of the material and the spiritual, drawing us closer to the unfathomable beauty and wisdom inherent in the cosmic tapestry.

Chapter XIX
SIGNS IN THE STARS

Historical Perspectives on Astronomy in Islamic Tradition:

During the Islamic Golden Age, there was a flourishing of scientific knowledge and advancements, with astronomy holding a prominent position in the pursuit of understanding celestial bodies and their movements. Islamic scholars made significant contributions to this field, building upon the knowledge inherited from ancient civilizations such as the Greeks, Babylonians, and Indians. The translation movement, notably the House of Wisdom in Baghdad, facilitated the transfer of scientific texts from different cultures into Arabic, allowing scholars to access and build upon diverse knowledge. One such example is the work of the Persian astronomer, Al-Battani (858-929 CE), who refined the measurements of the obliquity of the ecliptic and compiled improved astronomical tables. His influential work demonstrated the assimilation and advancement of astronomical knowledge within the Islamic world.

Islamic scholars also recognized the interconnectedness between faith and scientific inquiry, viewing the heavens as a testament to divine order and precision. This perspective led to a harmonious integration of religious beliefs with observational astronomy. Notable astronomers and polymaths such as Ibn al-Haytham (Alhazen) furthered this approach by emphasizing empirical observation and experimentation, laying the foundation for the scientific method centuries before its formal articulation in the West. Alhazen's comprehensive studies on optics and vision, including his groundbreaking work 'The Book of Optics', influenced scientific thought in both the Islamic world and Europe.

Astronomy played a crucial role in Islamic society, serving practical and religious purposes. The development of accurate astronomical calendars was essential for determining the precise times for prayer, fasting, and pilgrimage, thereby regulating important religious observances. Moreover, the construction of elaborate astronomical instruments like astrolabes and quadrant instruments allowed navigators and astronomers to make precise measurements of celestial objects, aiding in timekeeping, astrology, and navigation. It is through these advancements that Islamic astronomical tradition not only facilitated religious practices but also contributed significantly to the global body of scientific knowledge.

The Intersection of Faith and Sciences:

The Quran's portrayal of celestial bodies as signs of God's creation provides a foundation for contemplating the universe's mysteries. Surah Al-An'am (The Cattle) verse 97 states, 'It is He who made the stars for you so that you may be guided by them in the darkness of the land and the sea. We have explained our revelations in detail for people who understand.' This verse emphasizes the practical purpose of stars as navigational guides, emphasizing the Quran's relevance in guiding humanity through the natural world. Moreover, the Quranic verses do not merely offer utilitarian descriptions of celestial bodies; they also encourage believers to reflect on the design and order of the cosmos. Surah Ya-Sin verse 40 states, 'It is not permitted to the sun to catch up the moon, nor can the night outstrip the day. Each just swims along in its own orbit according to Law.' This eloquent depiction portrays cosmic harmony and precise natural laws governing the movements of celestial bodies, igniting contemplation on the divine wisdom underlying the universe's workings. Furthermore, the Quranic verses on celestial bodies provide an impetus for scientific inquiry. Today, scholars and researchers find inspiration in exploring the natural phenomena described in the Quran. The precise movements of the sun, moon, and stars described in the Quranic verses continue to intrigue astronomers and astrophysicists, engaging them in the quest to unravel the cosmos' secrets.

Stars as Beacons and Guides:

The use of stars as navigational tools can be traced back to ancient civilizations, where seafarers and travelers relied on celestial bodies for direction and orientation. The knowledge of the night sky allowed mariners to front on to oceans and traders to chart their courses overland, guiding them safely to their destinations. In the Islamic tradition, the importance of stars as beacons and guides is significant, reflecting not only practical utility but also spiritual contemplation. Ancient astronomers and scholars meticulously observed and documented the patterns and movements of stars, paving the way for a rich legacy of celestial navigation. The unique positioning and constellations of stars provided a celestial map for early explorers, shaping their understanding of the world and beyond. The reliance on stars as dependable markers in the dark expanse of the night sky fostered a connection between humanity and the cosmos. Through their association with navigation, stars became symbolic of guidance and resilience, weaving through cultural narratives and religious teachings. The Quran's allusions to the stars and their role in navigation further underscore the intertwining of faith and science, emphasizing the divine design inherent in creation. By studying the stars and using them as navigational aids, ancient civilizations recognized the balance between natural phenomena and human ingenuity. Their astute understanding of the night sky transcended mere practicality, delving into a deeper appreciation for the interconnectedness of the universe. This reverence for celestial bodies also offered a source of solace and wonder, inspiring awe and reflection. As we delve deeper into the historical significance of stars as navigational tools, it becomes evident that they served not only as physical guides but also as conduits for spiritual contemplation and philosophical inquiry. The legacy of stars as beacons and guides resonates across cultures, emphasizing the allure and immeasurable impact of these celestial luminaries.

Symbolism and Contemplation:

In the Islamic tradition, astronomical phenomena have carried symbolic significance that transcends their physical manifestations. The stars, moon, and celestial bodies have long been revered as metaphors for spiritual contemplation and insight. Within Islamic mystical traditions, such as Sufism, the study of astral phenomena extends beyond scientific inquiries to encompass a deeper quest for divine illumination. These mystical interpretations view the cosmos as a mirror reflecting the unity and grandeur of the divine presence.

Mystics and scholars have delved into the symbolism of astronomical events, attributing layers of meaning to eclipses, planetary alignments, and celestial movements. For instance, eclipses are often seen as potent symbols of hidden spiritual truths coming to light, representing the unveiling of esoteric knowledge and the dissipation of ignorance. The waxing and waning of the moon are frequently interpreted as allegories for the cyclical nature of human existence, with its recurrent phases of growth, fruition, decline, and renewal.

Moreover, Sufi poets and philosophers have drawn inspiration from the elegant dance of the constellations, weaving allegories that resonate with themes of love, longing, and transcendence. The twinkling stars are likened to the gleam of enlightenment, guiding seekers on their inward journey towards the Divine Beloved. Each radiant star becomes a metaphor for an illuminated soul, emanating light amidst the darkness of the night sky, pointing the way for pilgrims traversing the spiritual realm.

Furthermore, the mystical interpretations of astral phenomena intersect with cosmological reflections on the interconnectedness of all creation. In this worldview, each celestial body is perceived as a manifestation of the divine attributes, symbolizing qualities such as mercy, beauty, and wisdom. Contemplation of the stars and planets becomes a means of deepening one's awareness of the harmonious interplay between the seen and unseen dimensions of existence, fostering a sense of reverence for the Creator's infinite artistry. Through such contemplation, individuals are encouraged to align their inner being with the celestial order, aspiring to embody virtues reflected in the cosmic symphony.

Lunar Cycles and Islamic Practices:

The connection between astronomy and the Islamic calendar is a testament to the fusion of scientific observation and religious practices. The lunar calendar, which serves as the foundation for various Islamic rituals and events, relies on the moon's phases to determine the passage of time. The journey of the moon across the night sky not only marks the beginning and end of each month but also plays a crucial role in determining the timing of religious observances. This reliance on the lunar cycle harks back to the early days of Islam when astronomical knowledge was sought after and integrated into daily life. The lunar calendar's unique structure exhibits a deep reverence for celestial phenomena, embodying a harmonious relationship between cosmological patterns and religious traditions. Within this framework, the sighting of the new moon holds immense significance, serving as a testimony to the interconnectedness of spirituality and natural rhythms. Islamic scholars and astronomers dedicated themselves to studying lunar cycles, devising sophisticated methods to predict the appearance of the new crescent with remarkable accuracy. The subtleties of the lunar calendar also extend to the determination of Islamic months, such as Ramadan, when the observation of the new moon heralds the onset of the sacred month of fasting and spiritual reflection. Moreover, the lunar calendar imparts a sense of anticipation and contemplation, offering believers an opportunity to actively engage with the celestial theater that unfolds above them. In this way, the study of lunar cycles transcends mere scientific inquiry and becomes a conduit for spiritual mindfulness, fostering a connection to the cosmos. Embracing the lunar calendar reflects a recognition of the interwoven nature of astronomy and faith, underscoring the importance of celestial observation in shaping cultural and religious practices. Furthermore, the lunar calendar's influence extends beyond temporal measurements, encapsulating the essence of Islamic heritage and the legacy of celestial wisdom.

Nature's Clockwork:

The movements of the sun, the moon, and the stars form a grand cosmic clock, orchestrating the ebb and flow of life on Earth. In the Islamic tradition, the Quran alludes to the orderly nature of these celestial phenomena, inviting contemplation on the balance and beauty of creation.

Day and night, dichotomous yet harmonious, mark the cadence of earthly existence. The relentless cycle of sunrise and sunset symbolizes the ceaseless march of time—a testament to the regularity and constancy of the universe. It reminds us of the fleeting nature of our transient lives, urging reflection on the purpose and meaning of our fleeting moments. Moreover, the alternation of light and darkness offers spiritual analogies, illustrating the interplay of good and evil, knowledge and ignorance, and enlightenment and obscurity.

Beyond the daily rhythm lies the dance of the seasons, each heralded by distinct astronomical events. The solstices and equinoxes, determined by the Earth's axial tilt and its orbit around the sun, signal the cyclical transformations from spring to summer, autumn to winter. These celestial occurrences dictate agricultural cycles and cultural festivities, shaping human societies and fostering a deep connection to the natural world. Through observation of the heavens, ancient civilizations crafted calendars to harmonize with the heavens, culminating in the Islamic lunar calendar, which retains relevance in religious rituals and traditions.

Furthermore, the lunar phases, tied to the Islamic calendar, hold symbolic significance that transcends mere astronomical observation. The waxing and waning of the moon mirror the eternal themes of growth, decline, and regeneration—an allegory for the perpetual cycles of birth, death, and renewal that define human experience. The synergy between celestial movements and terrestrial occurrences demonstrates the inseparable link between the physical and metaphysical realms, inspiring introspection and reverence for the divine order inherent in the cosmos.

In contemplating the celestial temporal markers, we are beckoned to recognize the synchronicity of universal rhythms and our place within them. Acknowledgment of these grand celestial mechanisms fosters humility and mindfulness, grounding us in anappreciation for the grandeur and harmony of the natural world. It prompts us to honor the wisdom encapsulated in the stars, allowing their silent guidance to shape our endeavors and aspirations.

Stars as Inspirations for Human Endeavor:

Throughout history, humans have gazed upon the night sky and found inspiration in the stars. These celestial bodies, with

their glow and constancy, have served as metaphors for guidance and direction in numerous cultural and literary traditions. In the context of the Holy Quran, stars are revered as symbols of divine illumination and guidance for humanity's moral and spiritual journey. The Quranic verses that reference stars emphasize their role as beacons of insight and enlightenment, urging contemplation of the universe's wonders. This metaphorical significance extends beyond religious interpretation, resonating with the human quest for purpose and meaning. Stars have long captivated the human imagination, evoking a sense of wonder and awe. Their steadfast presence amidst the expanse of the cosmos offers a powerful analogy for resilience and perseverance. Just as the stars remain unwavering in their positions, individuals may draw strength from their unwavering commitment to their goals and ideals.

Additionally, the patterns and configurations of stars have inspired creativity and innovation in various fields, from art and literature to scientific inquiry and exploration. The notion of using stars as guides for navigation extends beyond physical journeys; it also carries symbolic weight in the realms of personal development and ethical conduct. The fixed laws governing celestial movements offer a foundation for principles such as reliability and ethical constancy, serving as a reminder for individuals to uphold their values with steadfastness and consistency. Furthermore, the interconnectedness of stars within constellations mirrors the inherent interdependence of human societies, highlighting the importance of cooperation and unity in collective endeavors.

In the contemporary context, the metaphor of stars as inspirations for human endeavor continues to shape cultural expressions and societal aspirations. From motivational speeches to educational curricula, the symbolism of stars is used to encourage ambition, resilience, and aspiration. In the corporate world, the concept of reaching for the stars embodies the pursuit of excellence and the drive to surpass perceived limitations, fostering a culture of innovation and progress.

Reflective Practices Amidst the Cosmos:

In Islamic tradition, the celestial bodies are seen as signs from Allah and as manifestations of His wisdom and omnipotence, offering insights for introspection and contemplation. Interpreting these signs entails not only understanding the physical phenomena of the cosmos but also delving into their symbolic and metaphysical meanings.

At the heart of interpreting signs in the stars lies the ancient practice of celestial navigation. Long before the advent of modern technology, mariners and travelers used the stars as reliable guides, charting their course across oceans and deserts with celestial maps etched in the night sky. The navigational prowess of ancient seafarers was not just a display of practical skill; it reflected a deep reverence for the cosmic order and a symbiotic relationship between humanity and the heavens.

In contemporary contexts, the symbolism of celestial bodies continues to inspire artistic, philosophical, and spiritual pursuits. Artists draw on the imagery of stars and galaxies to evoke a sense of awe and interconnectedness in their creations. Philosophers ponder the implications of an ever-expanding universe, contemplating humanity's place in the grand scheme of cosmic existence. Spiritual seekers find solace and enlightenment in the metaphorical interpretations of astronomical phenomena, using the language of the cosmos to articulate the ineffable dimensions of faith and divinity.

Chapter XX
THE CREATOR OF LIFE, DEATH, AND THE UNIVERSE

The Beginning of Time:

The Quran illuminates the concept that time itself began with the onset of creation, marking the inception of all existence. Its description of the universe's origin provides a framework for understanding time as an integral component of the cosmic design, intimately connected to the unfolding of creation. According to the Quran, the universe came into being through the divine command, as God declared 'Be,' and it became. This divine act brought forth time as a dimension inseparable from the fabric of the cosmos, encapsulating within it the continuum of past, present, and future. This Quranic portrayal prompts contemplation on the nature of time, transcending mundane perceptions and elevating it to a metaphysical concept. In exploring the Quranic perspective on the universe's origin, one encounters the notion of a primordial moment when time commenced its inexorable march, heralding the genesis of all that exists. This perspective invites reflection on the significance of time as a structured framework through which the divine plan unfolds, shaping the destiny of all creation. Additionally, the Quranic portrayal of creation's inception and the commencement of time underscores the coherence and harmonious orchestration characterizing the universe's existence. It elucidates the interwoven relationship between time and creation, emphasizing their inseparability and mutual influence. This Quranic exposition unveils time as a fundamental element interwoven into the tapestry of creation, governing its rhythms and orchestrating its evolution. Such contemplation generates a deeper appreciation for the interplay between time and the cosmic order, transcending temporal limitations to discern the dimensions of the divine design.

Life as a Divine Gift:

Life, as perceived from a spiritual lens, embodies a tapestry of divine benevolence and cosmic significance. It transcends mere existence, for it is a gift bestowed upon us by the Creator, intertwined with purpose and meaning that reverberates through the fabric of the universe. The Quran reverently expounds on the notion of life as a testament to God's omnipotence and wisdom, where every breath we inhale and exhale echoes with the whisper of the divine.

Life emanates as a unique opportunity for sentient beings to engage with their surroundings, to contemplate the marvels of creation, and to perpetuate the universal harmony envisaged by the Divine Architect. Its essence lies not merely in biological processes, but in the capacity to experience beauty, love, empathy, and spirituality. It encapsulates the moral responsibility to cherish and respect all forms of life, creating a harmonious confluence that reflects the wisdom of the Creator.

Furthermore, life serves as a conduit for the manifestation of virtues such as compassion, resilience, and altruism, fostering connections that weave the very fabric of societies and civilizations. It is within the realm of life that individuals are tested, their character forged through trials, and their actions resonating through eternity. Through this lens, every interaction, every choice, and every moment becomes a precious thread in the tapestry of human experience, interwoven with divine purpose and significance.

The understanding of life as a divine gift impels individuals to strive for nobility and moral elevation, acknowledging the sanctity of existence and the interconnectedness of all living beings. This pertinence is echoed throughout the Quran, emphasizing the duty to cherish, preserve, and protect life in all its forms, recognizing it as an embodiment of the divine presence. Therefore, life as a divine gift necessitates the pursuit of enlightenment, knowledge, and reflection, propelling individuals towards a holistic understanding of their place in the grand design of creation.

The Cycle of Life and Death:

Life and death are the dual forces that govern the very fabric of existence, forming an inseparable cycle that encapsulates the essence of the human experience. At its core, this perennial journey serves as a testament to the transient nature of life and the legacy of mortality. Within the fluidity of this cycle, lies the perpetual ebb and flow of creation, as every living being becomes entwined in the cosmic dance of birth, growth, decline, and eventual departure. It is within this relentless continuum that one can discern the interconnectedness of all living things, each bearing witness to the unfaltering rhythm of the universe.

The inevitable embrace of death illuminates the significance of life, infusing every moment with poignant urgency and unparalleled depth. At the heart of this cycle lies the immutable truths of impermanence and renewal, as each cessation paves the way for new beginnings, ensuring the perpetuation of existence in its most wondrous guise. Moreover, the contemplation of this cyclical process invites reflection upon the interplay between mortality and transcendence, as the inevitability of death becomes intertwined with the indelible mark of immortality etched upon the human spirit.

Notably, the cycle of life and death extends beyond the confines of individual experience and encompasses the pulse of the natural world, exemplifying the harmonious equilibrium that defines the rhythm of existence itself. From the verdant fields teeming with vitality to the serene depths of the oceans, from the majestic flight of birds to the gentle rustle of leaves –

each embodies the ceaseless flux of life and the silent reverence of departure. Additionally, this cycle permeates the celestial spheres, as galaxies are born and stars cease their luminous reign, only to be reborn in the cosmic tapestry, marking the celestial dynamism that mirrors the terrestrial experience. In accepting this eternal cycle, one can find solace in the realization that despite the ephemeral nature of individual life, the collective legacy endures through the ceaseless progression through time and space. Ultimately, the recognition of this continuous journey unveils the sanctity of life and the transformative power of death, elucidating the symbiosis that pervades the essence of existence.

The Universe's Architect:

As we contemplate the magnificence of the universe, we are compelled to acknowledge the design and impeccable order that permeate every aspect of existence. The cosmos stands as a testament to the meticulous craftsmanship and unfathomable wisdom of its Creator. From the unparalleled precision of celestial movements to the balance of natural phenomena, every facet of the universe exudes an awe-inspiring harmony that defies human comprehension. The symphony of galaxies, each in its predetermined orbit, and the orchestration of cosmic events with unfailing regularity unveil the design inherent in the cosmos. This grandeur speaks to a deliberate plan set in motion by the Creator, illustrating His boundless knowledge and mastery over all creation. The harmonious alignment of celestial bodies and the interplay of gravitational forces reveal the divine artistry that governs the universe, emphasizing the precision and orderliness that underpin its very fabric. Through the lens of science, we discern the existence of laws and fundamental constants that uphold the coherence and uniformity of the cosmos, further attesting to the meticulous design infused into its very essence. This fluid interplay of elements, phenomena, and forces manifests the perfect balance that sustains the universe, echoing the omnipotence and omniscience of its Architect. Contemplating the order and harmony in the cosmos instills within us a deep sense of reverence and humility, as we come to recognize our infinitesimal place within the grand tapestry of creation. It beckons us to ponder the universe and the underlying unity that binds its diverse components, inspiring awe at the splendid orchestration of existence. The universe's orderly nature serves as a source of reflection and contemplation, inviting us to marvel at the coherence and synchronization evident in its expanse. Through this contemplation, we are drawn closer to an appreciation of the Divine Intellect behind this wondrous creation, compelling us to acknowledge the limitless wisdom and foresight embedded in the cosmos.

Unseen Worlds:

The concept of unseen worlds opens up an inquiry into the dimensions that lie beyond our tangible reality. Such contemplation allows for a deeper understanding of the interconnectedness and complexity of the universe. In exploring the notion of unseen worlds, we are compelled to acknowledge the limitations of our sensory perception and embrace the idea that there exist realities that transcend the physical realm. This extends beyond the astral planes and invites us to consider the metaphysical dimensions that shape our existence.

The Quran elucidates upon the unseen worlds, emphasizing the existence of angelic beings and spiritual entities which operate beyond the bounds of human visibility. It describes a reality that is intertwined with our own, yet remains concealed from our immediate senses. The acknowledgment of these unseen worlds not only enriches our intellectual pursuits but also fosters a sense of humility, reminding us of the vastness of creation and the limitations of human knowledge. Additionally, the awareness of unseen worlds prompts introspection, encouraging individuals to strive for spiritual purification and moral rectitude in order to front on to these ethereal dimensions conscientiously.

Additionally, the contemplation of unseen worlds offers solace in times of adversity, as it fosters the belief in a broader, benevolent cosmic order that transcends the immediate challenges of earthly existence. In recognizing the existence of unseen worlds, individuals are prompted to expand their consciousness and embrace a holistic worldview that encompasses both the tangible and intangible aspects of creation. This expands our capacity for empathy, compassion, and understanding, as we acknowledge that the human experience intertwines with unseen forces and energies that shape our individual and collective destinies.

Divine Intention - Purpose Behind Existence:

The exploration of the divine intention behind existence invites contemplation on the purpose that underpins every aspect of existence, from the infinitesimal to the infinite, from the material to the ethereal. Central to this exploration is the notion of divine wisdom and foresight, wherein every entity, event, and circumstance unfolds within the overarching framework of a meticulously designed plan. This divine intention encompasses the interplay between free will and predestination, underscoring the balance of human agency within the scheme of cosmic orchestration.

Delving into the purpose behind existence leads one to ponder the ultimate aim of creation itself. It raises fundamental questions about the nature of reality, consciousness, and the intertwined destinies of all beings. The pursuit of this understanding offers insights into the unfolding of history, the evolution of civilizations, and the trajectory of humanity's collective journey. Moreover, it prompts an exploration of the ethical and moral dimensions inherent in the comprehension of divine purpose, as it guides individuals and communities towards pathways of righteousness and virtue.

In the context of the Quran, the divine intention behind existence resonates as a recurring motif, threading through the narratives of prophets, the exhortations for self-reflection, and the guidance for righteous conduct. It illuminates the interconnectedness of all creation and underscores the significance of striving towards the fulfillment of a higher purpose. Within this framework, the individual is called upon to seek alignment with the divine intent, acknowledging their place within the greater whole while pursuing personal growth and spiritual elevation.

The recognition of divine intention also fosters a sense of interconnectedness with the cosmos, engendering humility and awe in the face of the unfathomable intricacies of existence. It inspires a reverence for the sanctity of life, an appreciation for the beauty of diversity, and a responsibility towards stewardship of the earth and its resources. The divine intention serves as a guiding beacon, steering humanity towards enlightenment, compassion, and justice, anchoring moral frameworks and social systems in the principles of equity and harmony.

Matter and Spirit:

The synthesis of matter and spirit is an integral aspect of human existence, embodying the balance between the physical and metaphysical realms. At the core of this convergence lies the human consciousness, serving as the nexus where the tangible and intangible coalesce. Matter, representing the material form and substance, is inseparable from the essence of the human experience. From the moment of birth, individuals are enveloped in the corporeal world, facing its intricacies and engaging with its diverse elements. Simultaneously, the ethereal dimension of spirit permeates every facet of human life, imbuing it with purpose, emotions, and consciousness. This interplay between matter and spirit shapes the very fabric of human existence, forging a pathway towards understanding the interconnectedness of the tangible and transcendental.

The duality of existence, characterized by the coexistence of materiality and spirituality, underscores the complexity of the human condition. It prompts contemplation on the derived purpose, morality, and destiny within the broader tapestry of creation. Furthermore, the integration of matter and spirit unveils the interwoven nature of the universe, illustrating the interdependence and synergy that governs the cosmic order. In exploring this convergence, one is compelled to probe deeper into the mysteries of human consciousness, seeking to fathom the unity of the physical and metaphysical aspects of being. This journey of introspection delves into the mechanisms through which the mind and soul interact, offering insights into the inherent complexities of human nature.

On the other hand, the integration of matter and spirit resonates deeply within religious and philosophical discourses, with various traditions expounding on the harmonious coexistence of these two fundamental components. The symbiotic relationship between the physical and metaphysical dimensions serves as a cornerstone for moral and ethical frameworks, shaping individual beliefs and societal structures. Additionally, the integration of matter and spirit embodies the eternal quest for enlightenment and transcendence, encapsulating the human aspiration for spiritual fulfillment and existential meaning. The pursuit of balance between these dichotomous forces entails a journey toward self-discovery, wisdom, and inner harmony.

Guardian Role on Earth:

As observers, stewards, and trustees of the Earth, humanity holds a unique responsibility in preserving and nurturing the planet. The concept of vicegerency emphasizes that humans are entrusted with the protection and care of the natural world, recognizing it as a divine trust that must be upheld with diligence and wisdom. This noble duty calls for a harmonious relationship between human activities and environmental sustainability, reflecting the inherent balance and interconnectedness of the ecosystem. It underscores the imperative for conscientious stewardship, mindful consumption, and the prudent management of resources to ensure a flourishing and equitable coexistence for all life forms. Humanity's role as vicegerent is not merely one of dominion over nature but rather a sacred covenant to cherish, respect, and safeguard the Earth's web of life. Acknowledging this privileged position compels individuals and societies to adopt environmentally conscious practices, promote biodiversity, and foster ecological empathy. It also necessitates the pursuit of ethical and sustainable development models that honor the sanctity of the environment and uphold the rights of future generations. Embracing the mantle of vicegerency entails cultivating a sense of environmental ethics, instilling a collective commitment to conservation, and championing initiatives that mitigate the impact of human influence on the environment. By embracing this custodial role, humanity can aspire towards global harmony, ecological equilibrium, and a legacy of responsible custodianship for the well-being of present and future inhabitants of the Earth.

Mortal Constraints - Acceptance of Mortality:

Mortality, by its very definition, signifies the temporal quality of earthly existence. It serves as a constant reminder of the fleeting nature of our time on this plane of reality and compels us to contemplate the significance of our actions within the confines of our limited years. The awareness of mortality fosters a deep appreciation for the value of time, encouraging individuals to prioritize meaningful pursuits and relationships while recognizing the impermanence of these opportunities. Furthermore, the acceptance of mortality encompasses the understanding that each individual holds a finite place within the grand tapestry of existence. This knowledge instills humility and emphasizes the interconnectedness of all life, prompting individuals to consider the impact of their deeds and contributions. Moreover, the inevitability of mortality inspires introspection and contemplation regarding the legacy one wishes to leave behind. It imparts a sense of urgency to lead a purposeful life, defined by positive influence and meaningful endeavors that resonate beyond one's temporal presence. Conversely, the prospect of mortality can evoke fear and existential angst, prompting individuals to grapple with the uncertainty of what lies beyond the threshold of life. Yet, within the framework of acknowledging mortal constraints, there exists an opportunity for spiritual growth and a reassessment of one's values and beliefs. Cultivating a sense of acceptance regarding mortality transcends the realm of individual attitudes and extends to societal perspectives on aging, end-of-life care, and the commemoration of those who have departed. It encourages empathetic and compassionate engagement with those facing mortality, fostering environments of support, understanding, and dignity in the face of life's inevitable conclusion.

Chapter XXI
SATAN'S ROLE AND INFLUENCE

The Conception of Evil - Satan's Origins:

Understanding the origins of this malevolent entity is essential in comprehending human existence and the perpetual struggle between good and evil. In religious teachings, Satan's genesis is often portrayed as a counterpart to the creation of the divine order, a being whose defiance and arrogance led to his expulsion from grace. Islamic tradition portrays the figure of Iblis, who refused to bow before the newly created Adam, challenging God's authority and subsequently cast out of paradise. This understanding not only provides insight into the ethical dilemmas faced by humanity but also serves as a potent reminder of the eternal conflict between the forces of darkness and the pursuit of righteousness. By delving into the conception of evil and the origins of Satan, we are compelled to confront questions about the nature of sin, the fragility of moral fortitude, and the ultimate purpose of existence in a universe fraught with opposing forces.

Satan's Revolt:

In exploring the narrative of Satan's revolt, we are confronted with an archetypal tale of defiance against divine authority. According to the Quran, Satan's rebellion represents the epitome of arrogance and insubordination. His refusal to bow before Adam, the first man, is not merely an act of dissent, but a manifestation of hubris and disobedience. This significant act of defiance reverberates through the ages as a cautionary exemplar of the consequences that befall those who challenge the supremacy of the divine order. Satan's revolt epitomizes the struggle between free will and submission to the divine will, encapsulating the eternal tension between autonomy and obedience. The symbolic significance of this rebellion transcends its narrative context, offering insights into the nature of temptation, moral choice, and the dynamics of human consciousness. Examining Satan's rebellion provides an opportunity for introspection and self-reflection, probing the depths of the human psyche and the perennial conflict between virtue and vice. This pivotal event underscores the inherent moral complexity of human existence and invites us to contemplate the relevance of the age-old dichotomy between good and evil. The narrative of Satan's revolt serves as a moral parable, engendering contemplation on the fragility of ethical resolve in the face of seductive enticements and deceptive allure.

The Fallacy of Disobedience:

Disobedience, particularly in the context of divine authority, carries consequences that reverberate through cosmic realms. The fallacious belief that defiance of the divine will can lead to personal empowerment is a misconception perpetuated by the adversary, Satan. The Quran elucidates the catastrophic ramifications of succumbing to this fallacy. Disobedience not only disrupts the harmonious order established by the Creator but also leads to a distortion of one's ethical compass and spiritual detachment. The repercussions of disobedience are not limited to the individual; they extend to the broader human experience and even permeate cosmic dimensions.

When humans veer from obedience to the divine decree, they become susceptible to nefarious influences propagated by the adversary. This susceptibility opens the door to lies, deception, and temptation, which ensnare individuals in a web of moral and spiritual turmoil. The cosmic implications of disobedience are multifaceted, impacting the balance of the celestial spheres and contributing to metaphysical discord.

Beyond the immediate consequences, disobedience bears long-term repercussions that resonate throughout the tapestry of existence. It disrupts the natural flow of blessings and divine grace, creating barriers that obstruct spiritual growth and enlightenment. Furthermore, disobedience enkindles a ripple effect that extends to future generations, perpetuating a cycle of estrangement from the divine presence.

Understanding the fallacy of disobedience necessitates an appreciation for its overarching impact on the human condition and the interconnectedness of cosmic forces. By recognizing the grave cosmic implications of disobedience, individuals are compelled to exercise vigilance and exert moral agency in aligning their will with the divine. Embracing obedience engenders harmony within oneself, the broader human community, and the celestial spheres, fostering an environment conducive to spiritual flourishing and fulfillment of one's existential purpose.

Satan's Instruments - Lies, Deception, and Temptation:

Satan is depicted as the ultimate deceiver and master manipulator. This portrayal stems from the belief that Satan's primary tools in leading individuals astray are lies, deception, and temptation. In the context of the Islamic tradition, Satan is considered to be the source of all evil, constantly seeking to lure humanity away from the path of righteousness. Understanding Satan's instruments sheds light on the pervasive nature of his influence and the challenges it presents to individuals striving for moral and spiritual integrity.

Lies form the foundation of Satan's strategy, as he distorts truth and sows seeds of doubt. Deception, on the other hand, allows him to cloak himself in various guises and misleading appearances, making it difficult for individuals to recognize his presence and resist his influence. Through temptation, Satan exploits human vulnerabilities and desires, offering false promises and fleeting pleasures to lead them away from virtue and righteousness. The interconnectedness of these instruments highlights the complexity of Satan's approach in undermining human morality and faith.

Whether in the form of pride, greed, or envy, Satan capitalizes on human weaknesses, appealing to the innate struggles that individuals face in their pursuit of ethical and virtuous living. Recognizing and resisting these instruments necessitates a deep understanding of one's vulnerabilities, a firm commitment to truth, and unwavering moral fortitude. Furthermore, acknowledging the potency of these instruments provides renewed perspective on the eternal struggle between good and evil, challenging individuals to actively discern truth from falsehood and uphold their moral responsibilities in the face of adversity.

Human Freedom and Moral Responsibility in the Face of Evil:

In the context of the Islamic tradition, the presence of evil, often personified by entities such as Satan, challenges the ethical framework within which individuals exercise their autonomy and confront moral dilemmas. The theological discourse surrounding human free will and its interaction with the concept of evil has sparked philosophical inquiries and spiritual contemplation for centuries. Central to this discussion is the notion of moral responsibility—how individuals experience their choices and actions in the presence of temptation and deceit.

In monotheistic belief systems, the idea that humans possess free will, yet hold moral obligations to resist malevolence, forms the bedrock of ethical conduct. The balance between personal agency and adherence to virtue is a theme that permeates religious scriptures and philosophical treatises alike.

As such, this discussion prompts an exploration of the inner struggles individuals face when confronted with the allure of wrongful deeds or the influence of malevolent forces. Furthermore, it calls into question the nature of evil itself and its origins, examining how the interplay between human agency and external temptations shapes individual destinies and moral accountability. This contemplation also delves into the implications of personal accountability in the face of adversity, elucidating moral decision-making and the continuous battle against malevolence.

While the theological significance of human freedom and moral responsibility is deeply rooted in religious doctrines, these principles extend beyond the realm of faith to resonate within philosophical inquiries and ethical deliberations across diverse cultural and intellectual landscapes. The amalgamation of theological themes with contemporary ethical frameworks underscores the perennial debate surrounding the nature of evil and the moral obligations of humanity.

Chapter XXII
THE LEGACY OF ADAM AND EVE

According to Islamic belief, Adam and Eve are revered as the progenitors of humanity, created by the divine will of Allah. Their story, as narrated in the Quran, serves as a foundational archetype that underlines the nature of human existence, their relationship with their Creator, and the moral consequences of disobedience and repentance. The narrative of Adam and Eve elucidates important lessons about free will, accountability, divine mercy, and the perpetuity of human fallibility and redemption. Through critical reflection on this seminal tale, believers gain insights into their own trials, tribulations, and ethical responsibilities. The story of Adam and Eve establishes the paramount importance of humility, sincerity, and submission to God's guidance as central virtues for leading an upright life in accordance with Islamic teachings. This foundational account also underscores the essential qualities of empathy, compassion, and mutual respect in all human relations, attributing a universal significance to their legacy that transcends cultural, geographical, and temporal boundaries. The concept of Adam and Eve as the archetypal parents of humanity emphasizes the fundamental unity and equality of all human beings, irrespective of their diverse backgrounds, thereby promoting social cohesion, solidarity, and justice. Their story not only provides spiritual nourishment and ethical guidance but also imparts wisdom that enables individuals to front on to modern life with fortitude and wisdom.

Creation and Significance of Adam:

As the inaugural human, Adam stands as an embodiment of divine artistry and intention, carefully sculpted from the essence of clay and brought to life by the breath of the Almighty. His creation symbolizes the commencement of the human saga, signifying the elevation of mankind to a position of stewardship over the earth and its inhabitants. The Quran vividly portrays Adam's genesis as a testament to God's boundless creativity and capacity for shaping the very fabric of existence. Adam, imbued with intellect and agency, becomes a paragon of wisdom and moral responsibility, tasked with discerning right from wrong and facing the pathways of existence. The significance of Adam's creation reverberates through the corridors of history, marking the inception of mankind's unending quest for knowledge, virtue, and spiritual enlightenment. His existence serves as a beacon of hope and aspiration, beckoning humanity towards the pursuit of divine grace and understanding. Moreover, Adam's story encapsulates the perennial struggle between adherence to divine guidance and yielding to the temptations of earthly desires, weaving a narrative of resilience, repentance, and redemption. By delving into the depths of Adam's creation, we unearth insights into the nature of human consciousness, the dynamics of ethical decision-making, and the quest for spiritual harmony. Ultimately, the creation of Adam epitomizes the divine benevolence that bestows upon humanity the mantle of custodianship, as well as the solemn duty to uphold righteousness, compassion, and justice in the grand symphony of existence.

The Formation of Eve - A Companion in Eden:

According to Quranic narrative, the creation of Eve is interwoven with the story of Adam and the foundation of humanity. Described as the 'mate' or 'companion' to Adam, Eve's existence signifies the essential duality within human experience. Her creation from Adam's rib, symbolically illustrates the interconnectedness and interdependence of man and woman. However, it is crucial to recognize that the Quran emphasizes the equality and complementary nature of both genders, rather than the subordination of one to the other. The formation of Eve not only expands the scope of human existence but also underscores the significance of partnership and unity in fulfilling divine purposes. In Islamic tradition, Eve embodies wisdom, resilience, and strength, offering a different perspective from which to comprehend the nature of creation and the responsibilities placed upon humanity. The development of Eve's character and her role as a companion in Eden elucidates the Qur'anic message about the inherent worth and purpose of women in society and religious practice. Exemplifying the breadth and depth of Divine wisdom, the story of Eve encourages an interpretation that promotes reverence and appreciation for both male and female contributions to the human story.

Life in Paradise - The Original Blessing:

Life in the paradisiacal realm was characterized by an unparalleled sense of tranquility and harmony. Adam and Eve, the progenitors of humanity, were provided with an idyllic environment replete with boundless beauty and abundance. The verdant meadows, crystal-clear streams, and fruit-laden trees adorned the landscape, radiating an ethereal glow that transcended earthly splendor. Every breath was filled with the pure essence of serenity and contentment, enveloping the first human beings in a state of blissful rapture.

Amidst this symphony of perfection, Adam and Eve reveled in their unblemished connection with the divine. Their communion with the Creator was luminescent, a radiant bond woven with love and reverence. Their existence was embellished not only by the physical opulence of paradise but also by the spiritual elevation they experienced in the proximity of their Lord. Each day unfolded as a seamless tapestry of fulfillment and purpose, as they basked in the love and beneficence of the Almighty.

In the midst of this celestial opulence, Adam and Eve found solace in their reciprocal companionship. Their union was not just a convergence of flesh and spirit, but an intertwining of complementary beings, embodying the epitome of unity envisioned by the Divine. Their interactions emanated a harmony, resonating through the garden like the gentle whisper of a zephyr, affirming the inviolable sanctity of their union.

The bounteous provisions of paradise served as a testament to the Creator's benevolence and munificence. Every fruit bore the sweet nectar of gratification, every stream whispered tales of purity, and every glade offered respite from the turmoil of a world yet to be known. It was a realm suffused with omnipotent blessings, where the euphony of creation harmonized in reverent worship to its Maker, extolling His majesty and grace.

Thus, life in paradise epitomized the quintessence of divine favor, illuminating the splendor of existence and the intimacy of human connection with the Divine. It was a chapter of serenity and spiritual fulfillment, setting the stage for the events that would ultimately irrevocably alter the course of human history.

Prohibition and Temptation - The Forbidden Fruit:

In the idyllic setting of Eden, a paradisiacal garden blessed with abundance and serenity, Adam and Eve existed in perfect harmony with their surroundings. However, their felicity was destined to be tested by the ultimate trial – the temptation of the forbidden fruit. According to the Quranic narrative, God had clearly instructed the first human couple to partake of anything in Paradise except for a singular tree. However, Satan, in his malevolent cunning, lured them towards disobedience, enticing them with false promises of immortality and endless dominion. The allure of this forbidden fruit represented not only a physical indulgence but also a test of unwavering obedience and commitment to the divine command.

Amidst the lush foliage and glistening waters of the Garden, the temptation to defy God's decree proved overwhelming, and the fateful moment arrived as Adam and Eve yielded to their desires and consumed the prohibited fruit. Instantly, their blissful existence was shattered, and they became acutely aware of their transgression. Such an act was not merely an act of consumption, but a pivotal choice that irrevocably altered their destiny. As they bit into the forbidden fruit, they breached the divine covenant, inviting sin and mortality into their pristine world. Consequently, the once bountiful garden transformed into a realm marked by struggle and hardship, mirroring the internal conflict and turmoil within the souls of the first human beings. Their defiance against God's command ushered in the era of mortality and susceptibility to temptation, forever altering the course of human history.

As the forbidden fruit seeped into their consciousness, Adam and Eve were confronted with the weight of their actions. They experienced a sense of remorse, recognizing the grave consequences of succumbing to their desires. In the aftermath of their disobedience, they found themselves expelled from the confines of Paradise, exiled to the unfamiliar terrain of the earthly realm. This expulsion served as a poignant testament to the price of transgression and a solemn reminder of the indispensable nature of divine obedience. It symbolized the departure from the harmonious haven of Eden to a world fraught with challenges and trials, bearing the burden of their lapse with them. Their repentance echoed through the annals of time, exemplifying the intrinsic human capacity for seeking forgiveness and redemption in the wake of moral error.

The account of Adam and Eve's ordeal with the forbidden fruit serves as an allegory, resonating across generations and cultures, offering insights into human nature and the tests of faith and resilience. Their story underscores the perennial struggle between the sanctity of divine commandments and the allure of worldly temptations, embodying the balance between free will and divine guidance. Ultimately, the forbidden fruit represents a defining moment in the narrative of human existence, encapsulating crucial lessons about accountability, repentance, and the indomitable human spirit.

The Fall - Consequences of Disobedience:

The narrative of the Fall, representing the disobedience of Adam and Eve in succumbing to the temptation of consuming the forbidden fruit, holds significance within the Islamic faith. The consequences of this pivotal event resonate throughout human history and are integral to understanding the nature of divine commandments and the human condition. As Adam and Eve yielded to their desire and violated the explicit prohibition set by God, they experienced an irrevocable shift in their existence. This act of disobedience led to immediate repercussions, altering not only their own destiny but also reshaping the relationship between humanity and the divine.

The ramifications of this transgression were multi-faceted. Firstly, Adam and Eve's expulsion from the blissful abode of Paradise marked a definitive separation from the direct presence of God, initiating their terrestrial sojourn fraught with toil and hardship. Consequently, the allure of sin and the burden of mortality became intrinsic to the human experience, tainting the purity of the soul and engendering spiritual vulnerability. This rupture in the harmonious communion with the Divine illuminated the fragility of human agency and underscored the conflict between free will and divine ordinance.

Moreover, the Fall engendered a legacy of inherent imperfection and vulnerability within humanity, manifesting in the form of original sin. The moral inheritance of this primordial transgression permeates subsequent generations, shaping the proclivity towards wrongdoing and the perpetual struggle against the temptations that besiege the human conscience. It catalyzed a heightened awareness of moral culpability and the imperative quest for spiritual rectitude. Despite the weight of this legacy, the account of the Fall serves not only as a cautionary tale but also as a testament to the power of repentance and the promise of redemption.

Furthermore, the consequence of disobedience extended beyond the individual, casting a shadow over the dynamics of gender relations. Eve, in particular, has been subject to diverse interpretations regarding her role in the commission of the original sin. The implications of her actions have reverberated through cultural narratives and theological discourse, contributing to complex paradigms of female autonomy, accountability, and subjugation. The narrative of the Fall prompts contemplation on gender dynamics, agency, and the influence of archetypal depictions in perpetuating social constructs.

Repentance and Redemption:

Repentance, as emphasized in Quranic teachings, is the gateway to seeking divine forgiveness. It is an acknowledgment of one's mistakes and a sincere commitment to rectify them. The story of Adam and Eve serves as a powerful illustration of this fundamental concept. Their act of disobedience led to their expulsion from paradise, yet it also offered the opportunity for repentance and redemption. The Quran teaches that when Adam and Eve realized their error and turned to God in repentance, they were granted His forgiveness and mercy. This demonstrates the immense capacity for forgiveness within the divine essence, instilling hope and encouragement in the hearts of believers.

The process of seeking forgiveness involves genuine remorse, a firm resolve to refrain from repeating the transgression, and a request for God's mercy. In Islamic tradition, repentance is not merely a verbal expression but a transformative inner journey. It signifies a deep internal realization of one's wrongdoings and a sincere intention to mend one's ways. Through sincere repentance, an individual can attain spiritual purification and a restored sense of closeness to the divine. Moreover, the act of seeking divine forgiveness is not limited to personal transgressions but extends to repairing any harm caused to others. It emphasizes the reconciliatory aspect of seeking forgiveness, promoting harmony and empathy within the community.

The Quranic portrayal of repentance and forgiveness serves as a guiding light for believers, depicting the compassionate nature of God and His willingness to accept genuine contrition. It underscores the universal opportunity for renewal and transformation, regardless of past actions. By seeking divine forgiveness, individuals are encouraged to embrace humility, self-reflection, and accountability, fostering personal growth and the strengthening of ethical values. The narrative of repentance and redemption is a recurring motif in the Quran, conveying the overarching message of hope and mercy. It reaffirms the eternal potential for spiritual rejuvenation and the persistent invitation to return to God with a pure heart.

Legacy and Lineage:

As the first humans in Islamic teachings, Adam and Eve serve as the progenitors of all subsequent generations, symbolizing the shared origins and common ancestry of mankind. This lineage establishes a universal kinship among individuals, transcending geographical, cultural, and ethnic boundaries. The Quran elucidates this concept by emphasizing the inherent dignity and equality of all people, regardless of their backgrounds, through the divine declaration that "We have certainly created man in the best of stature" (Quran 95:4). This assertion underscores the foundational belief in the inherent worth and essential unity of humankind, rooted in the lineage of Adam and Eve.

Exploring the lineage of Adam and Eve unveils a rich tapestry of narratives, exemplifying the extensive diversity within humanity while reinforcing its underlying unity. Through the experiences of their descendants, the Quran communicates valuable lessons and wisdom about compassion, resilience, and the pursuit of virtue. These accounts offer insight into human nature, illustrating both the nobility and frailty of mankind. Moreover, the stories of Adam and Eve's descendants provide an ethical framework for understanding familial relationships, societal responsibilities, and the dimensions of moral conduct in diverse contexts.

By recognizing the lineage of Adam and Eve, individuals are encouraged to embrace their roles as stewards of the earth and custodians of future generations. This connection to the original ancestors engenders a sense of shared responsibility for the well-being of humanity and the preservation of the natural world. The narrative of human lineage thus becomes a guiding principle for promoting harmony, empathy, and conscientious stewardship among individuals and communities.

Chapter XXIII
PROPHETHOOD OF JESUS

Introduction to Jesus' Prophethood:

In Islamic tradition, Jesus is regarded as a distinguished prophet, bearing a divine message and a miraculous mission. The purpose of prophethood in Islam resonates with its broader function: to convey God's guidance, exemplify righteous conduct, and warn against moral transgressions to foster spiritual growth within societies. Through their teachings and exemplary lives, prophets serve as conduits for transmitting divine wisdom and exemplifying the highest standards of moral and ethical behavior. As such, Jesus' prophethood within Islamic tradition signifies an integral link in the chain of prophetic succession, marking him as an exemplary figure inspiring adherence to God's commandments and fostering spiritual growth.

Delving into the specifics of Jesus' prophethood unveils crucial insights into the unique aspects of his ministry and the divine messages imparted through him. Moreover, exploring the nuances of his mission offers an enriching opportunity to appreciate the convergence and divergence between Islamic and Christian perspectives on Jesus' role as a prophet.

In the Quran, Jesus, known as 'Isa' in Arabic, is revered as a prophet and messenger of Allah, emphasizing his miraculous birth to the Virgin Mary, his mission as a messenger to the Children of Israel with wisdom and miraculous signs, and his virtuous character as an exemplary servant of God. His story intertwines with that of other prophets, including Adam, Abraham, Moses, and Muhammad, forming an essential part of the Islamic narrative. One of the defining aspects of Jesus' presence in Islamic tradition is the emphasis on his human nature, devoid of any divine attributes or claims to divinity. Rather, he is celebrated for his piety, compassion, and mission to uphold the monotheistic faith. The depiction of Jesus in the Quran offers an alternative perspective to the narratives found in Christian traditions, highlighting his role as a humble servant of God rather than a deity incarnate.

Beyond the Quran, Islamic tradition further elaborates on the life and teachings of Jesus through Hadith literature, scholarly exegesis, and cultural expressions. Various accounts provide insights into his upbringing, ministry, disciples, and interactions with the society of his time. These sources offer a nuanced portrayal of Jesus within the broader framework of prophethood in Islam, shedding light on his esteemed position as a righteous and dedicated advocate for truth. Furthermore, the historical context encompasses the spread of Islam and its encounters with Christian societies, resulting in diverse perspectives and interpretations of Jesus' significance. This interaction has engendered vibrant discussions, debates, and mutual understanding between Muslims and Christians, shaping the evolving discourse on Jesus in Islamic tradition.

Miracles as Signs of Prophethood:

Miracles have long been considered as compelling evidence of prophethood, serving to validate the divine authority and legitimacy of prophets. In the context of Jesus' prophethood, his miracles are particularly significant, signifying his special status and connection with God. The Islamic tradition affirms that Jesus performed numerous miracles, each serving as a sign of his prophetic mission and divine approval. These miracles, ranging from healing the sick to bringing the dead back to life, demonstrated an extraordinary power beyond human capability, reinforcing Jesus' role as a prophet. His ability to perform such remarkable feats was indicative of his unique relationship with the divine realm. It is important to note that these miracles were not performed for mere showmanship but rather as demonstrations of spiritual truths.

Each miracle held a deeper meaning, conveying a message of compassion, mercy, and the power of faith. Moreover, the significance of these miracles lies in their ability to awaken people's hearts and minds to the reality of the divine. By witnessing these extraordinary acts, individuals were moved to acknowledge the existence of a higher reality and to contemplate the purpose of life. Furthermore, the miracles of Jesus exemplified the mercy and compassion of God, reminding humanity of the boundless love and care that the Creator has for His creation. They served as catalysts for spiritual awakening and transformation, leading people to draw closer to God and embrace righteousness and goodness.

Miracles also served to distinguish true prophets from impostors or false claimants. In the case of Jesus, his miracles were a clear indication of his authenticity and the divine origin of his mission. They set him apart from others and established him as a genuine envoy of God. The Quran attests to the miracles of Jesus, affirming their impact and extraordinary nature. The account of Jesus forming a bird from clay and then breathing life into it, as well as his ability to heal the blind and the leper, are cited as clear signs of his prophethood. Thus, the Quran emphasizes the miraculous nature of Jesus' mission, underscoring the undeniable evidence of divine support and endorsement.

Jesus' Message and Teachings:

Jesus conveyed a message of love, compassion, and righteousness to humanity. His teachings emphasized the importance of humility, forgiveness, and the pursuit of spiritual enlightenment. Jesus sought to guide people towards a closer relationship with God, emphasizing the inner purity of the heart and the significance of virtuous conduct. Central to his teachings was the concept of treating others with kindness and empathy, regardless of their social status or background. He promoted the idea of caring for the marginalized and vulnerable members of society, advocating for justice and equity.

In essence, Jesus' message transcended cultural and societal barriers, resonating with the universal values of compassion and righteousness. His emphasis on the ethical dimensions of human behavior and the pursuit of spiritual truth continues to inspire individuals across diverse faith traditions. Through his parables and sermons, Jesus imparted wisdom, addressing fundamental questions about the nature of existence, the human condition, and the ultimate purpose of life. His teachings underscored the transformative power of faith and the impact of living a life of integrity and compassion.

Additionally, Jesus' message emphasized the significance of sincere devotion to God, encouraging a deep and personal connection with the divine. His proclamation of the Kingdom of God and the call for spiritual awakening were pivotal aspects of his mission, instilling hope and renewal in the hearts of his listeners. Ultimately, Jesus' message and teachings exemplify a universal call for inner reflection, moral rectitude, and spiritual fulfillment, transcending temporal concerns and materialistic pursuits.

Differences Between Prophethood and Divinity:

The distinction between prophethood and divinity is a fundamental concept in Islamic theology, with significant implications for understanding the nature of Jesus as a prophet within the Islamic tradition. Prophethood, or 'nubuwwah' in Arabic, refers to the role of a chosen individual who serves as a messenger of God, conveying His guidance, laws, and instructions to humanity. Prophets are revered figures in Islam, and their teachings hold immense importance in shaping the moral, ethical, and spiritual framework of believers. On the other hand, divinity encompasses the concept of being divine or possessing the attributes of deity. In Islamic belief, Allah (God) is considered the only true deity, transcending all creation, and possessing absolute perfection and sovereignty. The notion of divinity is inseparable from the concept of tawhid, the oneness of God, which forms the cornerstone of Islamic faith. While prophets are exemplary individuals chosen by God to guide and instruct mankind, they are distinct from divine beings and do not possess inherent divine attributes. This clear differentiation between prophethood and divinity underscores the Islamic perspective on Jesus – acknowledging his esteemed status as a prophet, while firmly rejecting any assertion of his divinity. Understanding this distinction is crucial in elucidating the Islamic view of Jesus and preventing misconceptions about his role in the divine hierarchy.

Role of Jesus in Islamic Eschatology:

In Islamic eschatology, the role of Jesus holds great significance as it pertains to the end times and the final reckoning. According to Islamic tradition, Jesus will return to Earth prior to the Day of Judgment as a just ruler and a righteous leader. His return is believed to herald an era of peace and justice, marking the ultimate triumph of good over evil. This belief is deeply rooted in the Quran and Hadith, the recorded sayings and actions of the Prophet Muhammad.

The portrayal of Jesus in Islamic eschatology emphasizes his pivotal role in the unfolding of divine judgment and the establishment of justice. It reflects a reverence for Jesus as a revered prophet and a harbinger of hope in the face of adversity. Throughout Islamic literature, the return of Jesus is often depicted as a transformative event that will bring about a new era of righteousness and harmony. His leadership is seen as instrumental in guiding humanity towards spiritual enlightenment and moral rectitude.

Additionally, Jesus' arrival is believed to be a catalyst for the defeat of the false messiah (Dajjal) and the eradication of widespread corruption and oppression. Islamic eschatological narratives describe Jesus' mission in the end times as one of compassion, wisdom, and rectification. His extraordinary qualities as a compassionate healer, a peacemaker, and a defender of truth are revered as essential virtues that will shape the destiny of humankind. Moreover, his alliance with the Mahdi, a messianic figure in Islamic tradition, is anticipated to unite believers in a shared pursuit of justice and righteousness.

The teachings and principles espoused by Jesus during his return are envisioned to have an impact on global governance and societal ethics. In essence, the role of Jesus in Islamic eschatology is emblematic of the belief in divine justice and the eventual triumph of righteousness. It serves as a testament to the universal significance of Jesus as an exemplar of virtue and the embodiment of God's mercy and guidance.

Jesus in Relation to Other Prophets:

In the broader framework of prophethood within the Islamic tradition, Jesus holds a revered position as one of the mightiest messengers sent by God. His mission and teachings are linked to those of other prophets, establishing a cohesive narrative of divine guidance throughout history. Central to this narrative is the recognition of the common essence of prophetic messages across different eras and civilizations, despite their contextual differences.

The Quran underscores the interconnectedness of prophethood by emphasizing the universal message of monotheism and ethical conduct conveyed by all prophets, including Jesus. While each prophet was uniquely tailored to address the specific needs of their respective communities, the fundamental elements of calling people to worship one God and uphold moral virtues remained consistent. Hence, the role of Jesus stands in continuation of a tradition of prophetic succession, further corroborating the unity of purpose that defines the prophetic mission.

Understanding Jesus in relation to other prophets also illuminates the thematic threads that run through their teachings. Compassion, justice, humility, and resilience are recurring motifs in the stories of the prophets, including Jesus. By scrutinizing the commonalities in their narratives, an insight emerges: the shared struggle against adversity, the unwavering commitment to truth, and the relentless pursuit of righteousness. These parallels not only foster a deep appreciation for the collective wisdom of the prophetic legacy but also present a compelling case for the unified origin of divine guidance reaching its culmination in the teachings of Islam.

Moreover, delving into the coherence of prophetic missions offers a nuanced perspective on the significance of Jesus as a prophetic figure within the broader continuum of divine communication. His unique role as the Messiah and a beacon of hope for the oppressed resonates with the overarching theme of liberation and spiritual elevation prevalent in the stories of earlier prophets. Integrating Jesus into this larger narrative enhances our comprehension of the tapestry of divine revelation and the underlying harmony that characterizes the prophetic discourse.

Common Misunderstandings:

Misconceptions surrounding the prophethood of Jesus have persisted through the ages, often stemming from misinterpretations and varying theological traditions. One common misunderstanding revolves around the belief that Islam denounces Jesus altogether, when in fact, Islamic tradition regards him as a highly revered prophet. Another prevalent misconception is the conflation of Jesus' prophetic status with claims of divinity, which is a divergence from the core Islamic tenet of monotheism. This misunderstanding often arises from differing theological perspectives and can be clarified through an exploration of the distinct roles of prophets and divine beings within Islamic doctrine. Additionally, misinterpretations about the significance of Jesus' miracles and teachings in Islamic tradition contribute to misconceptions about his prophetic role. Further examination reveals that while Jesus is recognized for his miraculous deeds and teachings, these attributes affirm his prophetic calling rather than substantiate claims of deity. Lastly, the misconception that Islamic eschatology diminishes the significance of Jesus can be addressed through an in-depth analysis of his anticipated return and pivotal role in the ultimate divine plan.

Jesus' Death:

The Quran, considered by Muslims as the ultimate revelation of God's word, offers a distinctive perspective on the life, death, and purported resurrection of Jesus Christ. Through a tapestry of verses, it seeks to refute prevailing misconceptions while illuminating fundamental truths that transcend historical narratives.

Central to Quranic insights is the unequivocal assertion that Jesus was not crucified nor did he die on the cross. Instead, the Quran advocates the concept of 'tawaffa'—a term signifying natural death or a peaceful departure from the world. This pivotal revelation distinguishes the Islamic viewpoint from mainstream Christian beliefs and underscores the inherent theological divergence between the two faiths. Moreover, the

Quranic stance on the crucifixion is tied to the cosmic plan of God, emphasizing the inimitable sovereignty and wisdom governing His divine decrees.

Furthermore, the Quran meticulously outlines the essence of salvation within the Islamic framework, elucidating the concept of redemption through unwavering submission to the Almighty. It emphasizes the paramount significance of sincere repentance, virtuous deeds, and steadfast devotion as the pathways to attaining divine favor and eventual salvation. In contrast to the vicarious atonement doctrine prevalent in certain Christian doctrines, the Quran promotes individual accountability and spiritual autonomy as the bedrock of redemption—a paradigm shift that shapes the ethos of Islamic theology.

Quranic insights transcend mere theological discourse, encapsulating the universality of divine compassion and mercy. The Quran depicts Jesus as an esteemed prophet and exemplar of steadfastness amidst adversity, inspiring reverence and admiration across diverse religious denominations. In engaging with the Quranic revelations, we are endowed with an enhanced appreciation for the monumental impact of Jesus' legacy, serving as an interfaith bridge cultivating mutual respect and understanding.

Chapter XXIV
THE BROTHERHOOD OF HUMANITY

Human Unity:

In exploring the concept of human unity from a divine perspective, we encounter a truth that transcends cultural, racial, and religious boundaries. The Quranic perspective emphasizes that all of humanity shares a common origin and destiny, rooted in the divine creation of Adam and Eve. This foundational narrative reinforces the belief in the universal fraternity of humankind, echoing the interconnectedness and interdependence of the human family.

From a theological vantage point, the interconnected nature of humanity is woven into the fabric of creation, guided by the divine hand that shaped and sustained life itself. This understanding underscores the notion that regardless of geographical or ideological divisions, the intrinsic bond between individuals forms the basis of a shared human heritage. Moreover, it underscores the responsibility to uphold the dignity and rights of every individual as an essential component of a cohesive global society.

Approaching the topic through a divine lens illuminates the inherent connection that binds all people to a collective fate, fostering a sense of solidarity and empathy. This recognition nurtures an environment where compassion, mutual respect, and understanding thrive, transcending perceived differences and promoting harmony. The cosmic design espoused in the Quran reflects a tapestry of diversity, emphasizing that every individual constitutes a vital thread in the larger narrative of human existence. As such, the Quran directs attention to the moral imperative for individuals to recognize and appreciate the value of their shared humanity, affirming their interconnectedness as an eternal testament of the divine wisdom underlying creation. This reaffirmation not only underscores the sanctity of each individual life but also calls for a communal commitment to nurturing a society marked by inclusivity, tolerance, and equitable treatment for all.

Spiritual Cohesion:

The shared faith and common goals held by individuals across the globe form the foundation for connections and collaborations. This unity of purpose stems from the recognition of a higher, transcendent truth that resonates within the hearts of believers, guiding them towards collective endeavors rooted in compassion, justice, and righteousness. When diverse faith communities acknowledge their shared values and aspirations, a harmonious tapestry is woven, enriching society with a vibrant blend of perspectives and ideals. Moreover, this spiritual cohesion fosters an environment where mutual respect, understanding, and cooperation flourish, paving the way for peaceful coexistence and concerted efforts toward the betterment of humanity. The significance of shared faith and common goals is not confined to lofty theological discussions; rather, it permeates the everyday interactions and engagements of individuals, encouraging them to seek virtuous paths and to extend a hand of support to those in need, irrespective of differences. It inspires acts of altruism, benevolence, and selfless service, creating a bond that transcends the limitations of mere acquaintance or affiliation. Furthermore, this shared spirituality propels communities to work collectively towards addressing societal challenges, advocating for justice, and promoting the welfare of all. Through the lens of this unity, the richness of human diversity is celebrated as a testament to the inherent beauty of creation, fostering an inclusive environment that embraces the narratives and contributions of every individual. The intrinsic strength derived from spiritual cohesion empowers communities to stand in solidarity against adversity, comforting one another in times of hardship, and celebrating each other's triumphs as their own.

Social Harmony:

As individuals, communities, and nations intermingle on this shared planet, the cultivation of empathy and understanding becomes paramount in fostering genuine brotherhood across diverse cultures. Social harmony encompasses the recognition and appreciation of cultural differences, while simultaneously celebrating the intrinsic unity that underpins the human experience. It entails embracing the richness of diversity while forging bonds founded on mutual respect and compassion. At its essence, social harmony calls for the cultivation of an inclusive society where empathy transcends borders, ideologies, and prejudices. It requires a conscious commitment to bridge divides and nurture a spirit of universal kinship.

The concept of social harmony resonates deeply with the teachings of the Holy Quran, which emphasize the inherent dignity of every individual and advocate for the equality of all before God. The message of the Quran champions the idea of a global community united by compassion and justice, where the barriers of race, ethnicity, and social status dissolve in the light of shared humanity. Empathy and brotherhood form the pillars of this social framework, empowering individuals to look beyond superficial differences and connect on a level of understanding.

Through the lens of empathy, individuals can recognize and acknowledge the struggles, aspirations, and experiences of their fellow human beings, irrespective of cultural backgrounds or geographical origins. Such an empathetic approach paves the way for authentic relationships and harmonious coexistence in a world characterized by its mosaic of cultures and traditions. Cultivating empathy and promoting social harmony necessitate a commitment to fostering a culture of open communication, active listening, and genuine understanding. It involves creating spaces where individuals feel safe to express their unique identities, perspectives, and narratives without fear of prejudice or discrimination.

By nurturing an environment that values inclusivity and acceptance, societies can lay the groundwork for robust relationships built on trust, empathy, and respect. Moreover, social harmony engenders a collective responsibility towards addressing systemic injustices and advocating for the rights of marginalized communities. It prompts individuals to stand in solidarity with those who face oppression, inequality, and exclusion, working towards a unified vision of a world where fairness and equity prevail. In fostering empathy and embracing social harmony, humanity moves closer to realizing the innate interconnectedness that binds us all, transcending artificial divisions and cultivating a shared sense of purpose and belonging.

Equality Among Nations:

The Quran unequivocally emphasizes the fundamental unity of humanity, transcending all boundaries of nationality, ethnicity, and socio-economic status. The Quran repeatedly stresses the notion that all human beings are equal in the sight of the Divine, with no inherent superiority of one over another based on worldly criteria.

Surah 49, verse 13 states, 'O mankind, indeed We have created you from male and female and made you peoples and tribes that you may know one another. Indeed, the most noble of you in the sight of Allah is the most righteous of you. Indeed, Allah is Knowing and Acquainted.' This foundational verse underscores the intrinsic worth of individuals based on their piety and righteousness, rather than external factors. It promotes the understanding that diversity in cultures and societies is a means for mutual recognition and appreciation, not a basis for discrimination or prejudice.

Moreover, the Quran elucidates the equitable treatment of all individuals under Islamic governance, regardless of their origin or social standing. Surah 4, verse 135 admonishes, 'O you who have believed, be persistently standing firm in justice, witnesses for Allah, even if it be against yourselves or parents and relatives. Whether one is rich or poor, Allah is more worthy of both. So follow not [personal] inclination, lest you not be just. And if you distort [your testimony] or refuse [to give it], then indeed Allah is ever, with what you do, Acquainted.' This verse highlights the imperative of impartiality and fairness in judicial matters, emphasizing the preservation of justice without bias or favoritism based on lineage or economic status.

Mutual Respect:

The essence of mutual respect lies in acknowledging the intrinsic value of every individual, regardless of their cultural, ethnic, or religious background. It fosters an environment where differences are not just tolerated but celebrated, creating fertile ground for understanding and collaboration. The Holy Quran emphasizes the significance of mutual respect in fostering harmonious relationships among diverse communities. It calls upon believers to 'repel [evil] with that which is better' (Quran 23:96), advocating a response rooted in patience, kindness, and empathy. This approach is pivotal in transforming conflicts into opportunities for dialogue and reconciliation. Mutual respect, therefore, becomes the cornerstone for building bridges between individuals and nations, enabling the collective pursuit of peace and prosperity.

At its core, mutual respect is underpinned by an unwavering commitment to recognizing the dignity of every human being. It transcends partisan interests and political affiliations, serving as a unifying force in the quest for global harmony. The Quran illuminates the concept of respect through the example of Prophet Muhammad, who exemplified humility and compassion towards all, irrespective of their social standing. His interactions with people from diverse backgrounds underscore the universal applicability of mutual respect, offering a model for coexistence and cooperation.

Beyond individual interactions, mutual respect extends to the preservation of cultural heritage and traditions. By valuing and respecting each other's customs and beliefs, societies can weave a vibrant tapestry of diversity, enriching the collective human experience. This interconnectedness nurtures tolerance and understanding, dissolving barriers that breed mistrust and animosity. Through promoting mutual respect, communities and nations lay the groundwork for sustainable peace, resilient against the divisive forces of prejudice and discrimination. Moreover, mutual respect empowers individuals to transcend polarizing rhetoric and engage in constructive dialogue, fostering an environment conducive to diplomacy and conflict resolution. It compels leaders and citizens alike to seek common ground, discarding the shackles of intolerance and embracing the beauty of human plurality

Interconnectedness:

Interconnectedness encompasses the recognition that every individual, regardless of race, ethnicity, or creed, is linked through a network of mutual dependence and influence. This interconnectedness transcends geographical boundaries and cultural divisions, affirming the universal bond that binds us all as members of the human family. From the bustling city streets to the remote corners of the globe, each person's actions reverberate across this interconnected fabric, leaving an indelible imprint on the collective narrative of our species.

Whether through the exchange of ideas, trade, or humanitarian aid, the threads of interconnectedness intertwine to form a rich and complex mosaic of human interaction. In times of joy and celebration, these connections amplify our shared triumphs, uniting us in moments of elation and solidarity. Conversely, during periods of hardship and turmoil, the same interconnectedness calls upon us to extend support and empathy to those who bear the burdens of adversity.

The interwoven destinies of nations and individuals underscore the undeniable truth that no isolated action occurs within a vacuum; rather, it resonates throughout the interconnected framework of global society. Furthermore, recognizing the interdependence of humanity compels us to acknowledge the far-reaching implications of our choices and conduct, illuminating the responsibility each person holds in nurturing and preserving the vitality of this interconnected network. Embracing this understanding of interconnectedness fosters a culture of compassion, cooperation, and unity, serving as the cornerstone for fostering a world where every life is valued and every voice is heard. Consequently, the acknowledgment of our intertwined existence prompts us to strive for a more equitable and harmonious coexistence, grounded in the recognition of our shared humanity.

As we experience the complexities and challenges of the modern age, embracing interconnectedness empowers us to forge alliances, bridge divides, and cultivate a collective spirit of empathy that transcends the barriers that fragment our world. Ultimately, the realization of interconnectedness beckons us to stand in solidarity with one another, embracing the inherent dignity and worth of every individual as integral strands in the tapestry of shared lives.

Moral Responsibility:

The moral responsibility of humanity to uphold justice and compassion lies at the core of our existence as a global community. It is incumbent upon every individual, regardless of race, religion, or social standing, to champion the cause of righteousness and empathy. Throughout history, societies have grappled with the challenge of establishing equitable systems and fostering a culture of compassion. In the Quran, this moral duty is emphatically emphasized, outlining the imperative for individuals to act as beacons of integrity and mercy. Upholding justice means recognizing the inherent rights and dignity of all members of society, irrespective of their backgrounds. It entails holding oneself accountable for the fair treatment of others while striving to rectify injustices that plague our world. Similarly, compassion serves as the bedrock of harmonious coexistence, inspiring acts of kindness, understanding, and benevolence. It beckons individuals to extend empathy to those in need and to embrace diversity with open hearts and minds. The Quran articulates the interconnectedness of justice and compassion, heralding them as indispensable virtues for nurturing a thriving, equitable society. In contemporary times, the discourse on moral responsibility resonates deeply, given the prevalence of social inequities, oppression, and conflicts across the globe. It calls upon us to assume an active role in dismantling systemic injustices and advocating for marginalized communities. Furthermore, it demands that we cultivate a culture of understanding and inclusivity, ushering in an era of unity and mutual respect. To fulfill our moral responsibility, it is imperative that we confront the biases and prejudices that hinder progress towards a more just and compassionate world. We must engage in self-reflection, acknowledging our own shortcomings and biases, and strive to transcend them through education, dialogue, and proactive allyship.

Chapter XXV
THE ESSENCE OF FEARING GOD

The Concept of God-Fearing in Islam:

In Islamic tradition, the concept of fearing God goes beyond mere trepidation and apprehension. It delves deep into the psychological and spiritual makeup of a believer, emphasizing the foundational role it plays in shaping a devout life. The term 'God-fearing' encapsulates an attitude that is based on reverence, awe, and respect for the divine. It is not simply about cowering in fear of punishment, but rather about cultivating a consciousness of accountability and responsibility toward one's Creator. This concept serves as a guiding principle in every facet of a Muslim's life, influencing ethical conduct, moral decision-making, and spiritual reflections. Central to this notion is the acknowledgment of the absolute authority and transcendence of God, which engenders a sense of humility and submission. Furthermore, within the Quranic framework, the idea of fearing God is interwoven with love, hope, and trust, forming a multifaceted tapestry of devotion. It is about striking an equilibrium between veneration and adoration, grounded in a sense of duty and piety. Verses such as Surah Al-Imran (3:102) emphasize the concept of Taqwa, an Arabic term encapsulating fear, consciousness, and piety in relation to God. Additionally, the Quranic narratives recounting the stories of prophets and their encounters with divine manifestations illustrate the pervasive theme of fear and reverence towards God.

The Psychological Dimension of Fearing God:

In the Islamic tradition, the concept of fearing God encompasses a deep psychological dimension that influences the thoughts, actions, and attitudes of believers. This dimension goes beyond the mere apprehension of punishment; it delves into the workings of the human psyche and its relationship with spirituality.

At its core, the psychological dimension of fearing God involves an awareness of divine authority and accountability. Individuals who adhere to this belief recognize that their thoughts and actions are continuously observed by the Creator, fostering a sense of consciousness and mindfulness in their daily lives. This heightened awareness permeates every aspect of their existence, from personal conduct to interpersonal relationships, guiding them towards moral excellence and ethical behavior.

Moreover, the fear of God instigates an introspection of one's intentions and motivations. It prompts individuals to regularly assess their innermost thoughts and desires, discerning whether they align with the principles of righteousness and compassion espoused in the teachings of Islam. This self-accountability leads to a conscientious effort to uphold virtuous conduct, driven by the desire to attain spiritual fulfillment and closeness to the Divine.

Additionally, the psychological dimension of fearing God encourages believers to cultivate a sense of humility and awe in their reverence for the Almighty. This humility stems from acknowledging the inherent limitations of human knowledge and understanding, prompting individuals to approach their faith with reverence and deference. This conscious acknowledgment of human fallibility inspires a sense of awe and wonder, fostering an attitude of submission and reliance on the wisdom and guidance provided by divine revelation.

Furthermore, the fear of God serves as a catalyst for inner transformation, prompting individuals to confront their innermost fears, insecurities, and weaknesses. By acknowledging their vulnerabilities in the face of divine omnipotence, individuals are propelled towards self-improvement and growth, as they seek to overcome their shortcomings and strive towards embodying the virtues advocated in Islam. This transformative process nurtures a resilient and steadfast spirit, fortifying individuals against temptations and adversities encountered on their spiritual journey.

The Incentive for Moral Behavior through Fear:

The fear of God is not meant to instill a paralyzing terror, but rather to encourage conscious mindfulness of one's actions and their consequences. This fear acts as a deterrent against transgressions and wrongful deeds, fostering a sense of accountability and responsibility in the individual. By recognizing the presence and omniscience of the Divine, believers are motivated to align their conduct with virtuous standards and refrain from engaging in activities that contravene the teachings of Islam. This incentive highlights the integral role of fear in shaping ethical conduct within the Islamic framework. It underscores the significance of self-discipline and moral rectitude, underpinned by a reverence for the Almighty. Moreover, the fear of divine retribution compels individuals to act in a manner that reflects humility, piety, and integrity in all aspects of their lives. This incentive transcends the confines of personal morality and extends to nurturing a just and compassionate society, built upon principles of righteousness and mutual respect. Consequently, the fear of God becomes a catalyzing force for the pursuit of justice, equity, and benevolence, serving as a guiding beacon for individuals and communities alike. It prompts introspection and self-evaluation, encouraging continuous striving towards righteousness and moral elevation.

Balancing Fear and Love in Worship:

While fear of God serves as a crucial motivator for moral behavior and spiritual growth, this fear must coexist with love and adoration for the Almighty. The Quran emphasizes the need for believers to approach worship with both reverence and affection, acknowledging the awe-inspiring power of Allah while also nurturing a deep, intimate connection with Him. This duality forms the foundation of a reverent yet loving relationship between the worshipper and the worshipped. Striking this balance is essential in order to develop a comprehensive and holistic understanding of Islamic worship. It allows individuals to draw inspiration from the fear of divine retribution while simultaneously seeking solace and comfort in the boundless love and mercy of God. By embracing both emotions, Muslims can cultivate a more meaningful spiritual experience.

The fear of God instills a sense of accountability and responsibility, prompting believers to adhere to virtuous conduct and resist temptations that may lead them astray. Simultaneously, love for God fosters an emotional attachment that encourages devotion, gratitude, and a deep-rooted sense of belonging within the Islamic faith. As a result, worship becomes a dynamic interplay between awe and affection, guiding adherents to front on to life's challenges with steadfastness and humility while basking in the warmth of divine compassion. This harmonious fusion of fear and love elevates the worshipper's spiritual journey, fostering a comprehensive and nuanced relationship with the Divine that transcends mere ritualistic practice.

In integrating both fear and love into their worship, Muslims enrich their spiritual lives, manifesting an interconnectedness between the human spirit and the transcendental. This balanced approach provides believers with a holistic framework for spiritual growth and ethical conduct, underscoring the reciprocity inherent in the relationship between humans and the

Divine. Ultimately, by honoring the equilibrium of fear and love in worship, individuals can attain a deeper understanding of the intrinsic beauty and wisdom woven into the fabric of Islamic teachings.

Fear as a Motivator for Spiritual Growth:

In Islam, fear of God is often described as a motivator for spiritual growth and moral conduct. The recognition of divine accountability and the concept of 'Taqwa' (God-consciousness) serve as foundational principles to guide believers in their journey towards self-improvement. Fear, in this context, is not meant to instill dread or terror, but rather to inspire a sense of reverence and mindfulness of one's actions. This sentiment of awe and respect cultivates a mindset of humility and introspection, prompting individuals to constantly evaluate their deeds and intentions. As a result, fear becomes a driving force behind the pursuit of righteousness and ethical behavior.

Embracing fear as a motivator for spiritual growth encourages believers to be mindful of their conduct in both personal and communal settings. It serves as a reminder that every action, whether public or private, holds significance in the eyes of the divine. Consequently, individuals are propelled to engage in acts of kindness, charity, and compassion, seeking to alleviate the suffering of others and uphold justice in society. Fear, therefore, becomes a catalyst for positive change, inspiring individuals to uphold moral values and pursue excellence in their character.

Furthermore, fear as a motivator for spiritual growth fosters an environment of constant self-improvement and introspection. It provides the impetus for believers to seek knowledge, engage in acts of worship, and develop a deeper understanding of their faith. Through this lens, fear becomes a source of inspiration for continuous learning and spiritual enhancement, propelling individuals towards a state of increased awareness and mindfulness in their daily lives.

While fear may offer impetus for growth, it also intertwines with love in the realm of worship and devotion. The amalgamation of fear and love creates a harmonious balance, wherein fear motivates conscientiousness and love fosters a deep emotional connection with the Divine. This duality of emotion infuses worship with sincerity and fervor, allowing believers to approach their spiritual journey holistically, with both a reverent heart and an affection for the Almighty.

Common Misconceptions about Fear in Islam:

Misconceptions are a common occurrence when it comes to the understanding of fear in the context of Islam. One of the most prevalent misconceptions is the belief that fear in Islam induces a state of perpetual terror and anxiety. This notion is far from the truth. Islamic teachings emphasize a healthy fear of God that is rooted in reverence and awe, rather than a paralyzing dread. It is important for individuals to understand that the fear of God in Islam serves as a mechanism for self-discipline and spiritual growth, rather than a tool for instilling constant anguish.

Another misconception is the conflation of fear with blind obedience. In Islam, fear is not meant to coerce individuals into submission without question. Rather, it is intended to inspire humility and consciousness of one's actions. The fear of God compels believers to act with sincerity and righteousness, encouraging them to make conscious choices that align with their values and moral compass.

Additionally, there is a widespread misunderstanding regarding the balance between fear and love in Islamic practice. Some mistakenly perceive fear and love as conflicting emotions, failing to recognize that they can coexist harmoniously within the framework of faith. Islam encourages a holistic approach to spirituality, where respect and love for the Divine are complemented by a conscientious awareness of accountability and consequences. Understanding the interplay between these emotions is crucial in dispelling the misconception that fear negates the presence of love in Islamic teachings.

Furthermore, the misinterpretation of fear as a means of imposing authoritarian control is a distortion of its true essence in Islam. The fear of God is not wielded as a tool of domination by religious authorities; rather, it is a personal and introspective sentiment that guides individual behavior and moral choices. It serves as a reminder of the inherent accountability that each person bears for their actions, emphasizing personal agency and responsibility.

Chapter XXVI
REPENTANCE

Repentance, known as 'Taubah' in Arabic, holds a central position in the spiritual and ethical framework of Islam. It is a multifaceted concept that encompasses psychological, emotional, and behavioral aspects, deeply intertwined with an individual's relationship with the divine. In the Islamic context, repentance is not merely seeking forgiveness for specific actions or transgressions; rather, it signifies a reorientation of the self towards God, characterized by genuine remorse and a firm resolve to abandon sinful behavior.

The significance of repentance in Islam can be traced back to its foundational belief in the mercy and compassion of Allah (God). The Quran, the holy book of Islam, repeatedly emphasizes the boundless nature of God's forgiveness, providing believers with hope and encouragement to seek repentance regardless of the severity of their past transgressions. The act of repentance is also seen as a manifestation of humility and recognition of human fallibility, highlighting the egalitarian nature of the Islamic ethos that acknowledges the universal capacity for both virtue and vice.

From a psychological perspective, the process of repentance in Islam offers a means of introspection and self-improvement. By acknowledging and taking responsibility for one's wrongdoings, individuals engage in a constructive dialogue with their conscience, fostering a sense of moral accountability and personal growth. This internal transformation is guided by the Islamic principle of 'Taqwa,' or God-consciousness, which encourages adherents to develop heightened awareness of their actions and intentions, leading to a more discerning and principled approach to life.

Furthermore, repentance serves as a powerful avenue for rectifying interpersonal relationships and societal dynamics. Islam places great emphasis on the restoration of rights and the reconciliation of conflicts following repentance. This process underscores the interconnectedness of individual conduct and communal harmony, thereby reinforcing the ethic of social responsibility within the fabric of Islamic ethics. In essence, embracing repentance entails a commitment to strive for virtuous conduct not only in relation to the divine but also in the realm of human interactions, promoting justice, empathy, and goodwill.

The Psychological and Spiritual Dimensions of Repentance:

From a psychological perspective, repentance serves as a cathartic experience that allows individuals to acknowledge and confront their mistakes, remorse, and feelings of guilt. This process not only provides emotional relief but also cleanses the mind of negative thoughts and emotions, promoting mental well-being and inner peace. Moreover, the act of seeking forgiveness fosters self-reflection, leading to personal growth and development.

On a spiritual level, repentance represents a fundamental aspect of the relationship between an individual and their Creator. It signifies recognizing one's transgressions against divine commandments and seeking absolution from the Most Merciful. Through repentance, believers acknowledge their innate fallibility and dependence on divine guidance, thereby strengthening their connection with God. This spiritual component of repentance is deeply rooted in the concept of accountability and the striving for spiritual purification.

Furthermore, repentance is intertwined with the Islamic principle of 'Tawheed,' which underscores the belief in the Oneness of God and His attributes. By turning towards repentance, individuals realign themselves with their faith and affirm their commitment to the monotheistic principles upheld in Islam. This reaffirmation of faith can have an impact on the spiritual well-being of the repentant, fostering a sense of closeness to the Divine and an enhanced spiritual consciousness.

In addition to its psychological and spiritual implications, repentance plays a pivotal role in shaping the moral fiber of society. As individuals seek repentance for their wrongdoings, they contribute to the cultivation of a virtuous and conscientious community. The practice of repentance encourages humility, empathy, and accountability, thereby fostering a culture of forgiveness and compassion among believers. These collective spiritual values are instrumental in nurturing a harmonious and morally upright society, promoting mutual respect and understanding across diverse communities.

Conditions for Sincere Repentance:

Repentance holds a central place in Islamic teachings, emphasizing the mercy and forgiveness of Allah towards His creations. The Quran and Hadith offer invaluable insights into the conditions necessary for sincere repentance, guiding believers towards a deeper understanding of this spiritual practice. According to Islamic tradition, sincere repentance comprises several essential elements as outlined in the Quran and Hadith.

First and foremost, genuine remorse is fundamental to repentance. The individual must truly regret and feel deep sorrow for their wrongful actions or transgressions. This internal anguish serves as a catalyst for seeking forgiveness and signifies a genuine desire to rectify one's conduct. Such remorse is not merely a superficial acknowledgment of wrongdoing but a heartfelt recognition of having strayed from the path of righteousness.

Moreover, repentance necessitates the cessation of the sinful behavior. A true penitent must demonstrate a resolute commitment to abandoning the actions or attitudes that led to transgression. This requires a conscious effort to break free from the destructive patterns and to replace them with virtuous conduct. The Quran underscores the importance of actively shunning past misdeeds and embracing a renewed way of life rooted in piety and virtue.

Furthermore, genuine repentance requires an unwavering determination to amend one's ways. It is not confined to a mere verbal expression of remorse but extends to a steadfast resolve to reform one's character and uphold righteousness. This entails proactive steps towards self-improvement, seeking to enhance one's moral and spiritual standing in light of past failings. The Hadith emphasizes the significance of sincere intention and persistent effort as vital components of authentic repentance.

Additionally, seeking forgiveness from Allah through earnest supplication and prayer is indispensable to the process of repentance. The Quran encourages believers to turn humbly to Allah, acknowledging their faults and seeking His divine pardon. This act of humility and submission fosters a deep connection with the Almighty and reflects the believer's reliance on His mercy and benevolence. Genuine repentance involves a transformation of the inner self through constant supplication and seeking of divine forgiveness.

Finally, a crucial aspect of sincere repentance lies in making restitution and seeking reconciliation with those who may have been wronged by one's actions. This embodies the concept of accountability and demonstrates a genuine commitment to repairing the harm caused by one's transgressions. Both the Quran and Hadith underscore the importance of acknowledging and addressing the repercussions of one's misdeeds, thereby emphasizing the comprehensive nature of sincere repentance.

Barriers to Genuine Repentance and Overcoming Them:

Genuine repentance is a transformative process that requires introspection, sincerity, and a steadfast commitment to change. However, the journey towards repentance is often hindered by various barriers that can impede one's spiritual progress. Identifying and overcoming these barriers is crucial for individuals seeking genuine repentance and spiritual liberation.

One of the most common barriers to genuine repentance is the influence of societal and cultural norms. In some communities, seeking forgiveness may be stigmatized or viewed as a sign of weakness, leading individuals to suppress their remorse and avoid seeking repentance. Overcoming this barrier requires redefining the narrative around repentance and fostering an environment of compassion and understanding.

Another significant barrier is the struggle with ego and pride. Admitting wrongdoing and taking accountability can be challenging, especially when confronted with the fear of judgment or loss of reputation. Overcoming this barrier necessitates humility and self-reflection, acknowledging that true strength lies in the ability to acknowledge one's mistakes and strive for personal growth.

Furthermore, the lack of self-forgiveness can act as a substantial impediment to genuine repentance. Individuals may find themselves trapped in a cycle of shame and guilt, unable to grant themselves the same compassion and forgiveness they seek from the Divine. Overcoming this barrier involves practicing self-compassion and recognizing that everyone is deserving of redemption.

Additionally, external influences such as negative peer pressure or entrenched habits can create obstacles on the path to repentance. Breaking free from detrimental patterns and surrounding oneself with positive support systems are essential steps towards overcoming these obstacles.

To overcome these barriers, individuals must cultivate a mindset of resilience, perseverance, and self-awareness. Seeking guidance from mentor figures, engaging in moral self-inventory, and aligning actions with virtuous principles can aid in transcending these hindrances. Embracing a supportive community that values accountability and personal growth can also play a pivotal role in facing these barriers to genuine repentance.

Overcoming these barriers is not merely an individual endeavor but a collective responsibility within the community. By fostering an environment that encourages openness, vulnerability, and compassion, individuals can collectively address and surmount the barriers to genuine repentance, paving the way for spiritual growth and inner transformation.

Examples from the Lives of Prophets and Companions:

Throughout Islamic history, the lives of prophets and companions have served as examples of genuine repentance and its transformative impact on the soul. One such compelling case study is that of Prophet Adam (peace be upon him), whose story in the Quran illustrates the human experience of making a mistake, feeling remorse, seeking God's forgiveness, and experiencing spiritual growth. Although Adam initially disobeyed God by eating from the forbidden tree, he repented sincerely, turned back to God, and was ultimately forgiven. This narrative carries an essential message for believers— no matter how grave the sin, sincere repentance leads to divine mercy and redemption.

Likewise, the story of Prophet Yunus (Jonah) in the Quran offers valuable insights into the power of repentance. After initially abandoning his mission out of frustration, Yunus found himself in the belly of a whale. It was there, in the depths of darkness and despair, that he earnestly repented and sought God's help. Subsequently, he was saved from the whale's belly, and his repentance was accepted. This example teaches us that even in the most desperate circumstances, turning to God in sincere repentance can lead to miraculous outcomes.

The life of the beloved companion, Umar ibn Al-Khattab, serves as a noteworthy case study of repentance and transformation. Before embracing Islam, Umar was known for his strong opposition to the faith and his fierce temper. However, after professing the shahada and repenting for his past actions, he underwent a change. His repentance led to a remarkable transformation, and he became one of the most steadfast supporters of the faith, eventually succeeding Abu Bakr as the second caliph. Umar's example demonstrates that sincere repentance has the power to completely alter one's character and trajectory in life.

Furthermore, the story of Ma'iz ibn Malik, a companion of the Prophet Muhammad (peace be upon him), provides a touching illustration of repentance and the compassionate approach of the Prophet towards those who seek forgiveness. Ma'iz confessed to committing adultery and insisted on being purified through the prescribed punishment. However, the Prophet Muhammad displayed immense empathy and advised him to seek God's forgiveness. By pardoning Ma'iz and emphasizing the value of sincere repentance over severe punishment, the Prophet demonstrated the mercy inherent in the process of seeking forgiveness.

The Transformative Power of Repentance on the Soul:

Repentance is not merely seeking forgiveness for one's transgressions but also encompasses a deep transformation of the soul and a return to one's true essence. The transformative power of repentance is rooted in the belief that sincere remorse and a firm resolve to change can elevate an individual to a higher spiritual state. This process involves acknowledging one's faults, seeking forgiveness from the Most Merciful, and committing to righteous actions henceforth.

In Islam, the concept of repentance extends far beyond the act of seeking pardon for specific misdeeds. It reflects a fundamental shift in the inner being of the individual—a departure from a life characterized by heedlessness and sin towards one governed by consciousness, virtue, and devotion. The act of repentance serves as a catalyst for personal growth, spiritual renewal, and a reorientation towards the divine purpose.

The transformative power of repentance lies in its ability to purify the heart and mind. By acknowledging and seeking forgiveness for past mistakes, the individual cultivates humility and self-awareness. This introspective process not only leads to the resolution of immediate wrongdoings but also initiates a journey of self-improvement and refinement. Through genuine repentance, individuals confront their weaknesses, confront their weaknesses, transcend their shortcomings, and strive to embody the values espoused by the Quran and Sunnah.

Moreover, repentance instills a sense of accountability and responsibility in the believer. By taking ownership of their actions and seeking absolution from the Almighty, individuals actively engage with the ethical teachings of Islam, fostering a conscious awareness of right and wrong. This heightened consciousness guides them in making choices that align with their moral compass, thereby shaping their character and contributing to their overall development.

Additionally, the transformative power of repentance resonates through the emotional and psychological catharsis it offers. It provides solace and relief to the repentant soul, lifting the burden of guilt and regret. This release enables individuals to liberate themselves from the shackles of their past misdeeds and empowers them to embrace a future marked by hope, determination, and optimism. As a result, repentance not only serves as a means of seeking divine forgiveness but also as a source of inner peace and emotional healing.

The Role of Prayer and Worship in Reinforcing Repentance:

In the Islamic tradition, prayer, or Salah in Arabic, is a direct form of communication with the Almighty. Through the act of prayer, individuals not only seek forgiveness for their past transgressions but also commit to a path of righteousness and obedience. The five daily prayers serve as constant reminders of one's duties towards God and fellow human beings, thereby encouraging introspection, self-improvement, and repentance.

Furthermore, the ritual prostration (Sujood) in prayer signifies humility and submission before Allah, allowing individuals to shed their ego and seek divine mercy. This physical act of bowing down serves as a powerful manifestation of repentance, as it symbolizes surrendering one's shortcomings and seeking divine guidance and forgiveness. Additionally, the recitation of Quranic verses during prayer acts as a source of moral and spiritual awakening, reminding individuals of the consequences of their actions and the need for sincere repentance.

In addition to formal prayer, voluntary acts of worship, such as night prayers (Tahajjud) and supplications (Dua), provide opportunities for individuals to engage in deeper reflection and seek forgiveness for their sins. These acts not only reinforce the concept of repentance but also nurture a spiritual connection with the Divine, fostering a sense of accountability and gratitude. Dedicating time for intimate conversations with God allows for an exploration of one's inner state, paving the way for heartfelt repentance and a renewed commitment to virtuous living.

Moreover, engaging in acts of charity and service to others, which are integral components of worship in Islam, reinforces the process of repentance by emphasizing compassion, empathy, and social responsibility. By extending kindness and support to those in need, individuals not only seek atonement for their past wrongdoings but actively contribute to the betterment of society, aligning their actions with the principles of faith and repentance.

Chapter XXVII
ADULTERY AND IDOLATRY

Adultery - Quranic Perspective and Spiritual Consequences:

Adultery, as perceived through the lens of Quranic teachings, encompasses a broader spectrum than mere physical infidelity or betrayal. The Quran's standpoint on adultery is grounded in the notion of violating the sacred bond of marriage and the ethical implications thereof. From a Quranic perspective, adultery is not just an infringement of marital fidelity, but a disruption of the divine order and a transgression against the sanctity of the family unit.

The terminology used in the Quran to address adultery reflects its gravity and moral repugnance. The Quran employs precise language to depict the severity of engaging in adulterous behavior. By delving into the Quranic terminology related to adultery, one encounters expressions that underscore the gravity of such actions, emphasizing the consequential impact on both individuals and society at large.

Moreover, the Quran's definition of adultery goes beyond the physical act and delves into the psychological, emotional, and spiritual dimensions of this transgression. It elucidates how the ramifications of adultery extend beyond immediate participants and cast implications on social harmony, familial stability, and individual well-being.

On the other hand, adultery, as considered in Islamic teachings, is not only a violation of moral and ethical boundaries, but also bears spiritual consequences for the individuals involved. Quranic scriptures emphasize that engaging in illicit relationships and sexual impropriety disrupts the sacred institution of marriage, leading to erosion of trust, betrayal, and disharmony within the family unit. The severity of these consequences extends beyond the immediate impact on individuals and families, permeating through societal structures and moral fabric.

From the perspective of spiritual well-being, adultery represents a deviation from the prescribed path of righteousness and purity. It introduces impurity into the individual's soul and distances them from the divine presence of God. The act of adultery tarnishes the spiritual state of a person, causing a misalignment with the values and virtues upheld by Islamic principles.

Furthermore, the Quran underlines that engaging in forbidden intimate relations can lead to severe repercussions in the hereafter. It is believed that those who willingly persist in this transgression without seeking repentance may face dire consequences in the afterlife, thereby risking their eternal salvation. The spiritual implications of adultery are not confined to its immediate impact but extend to the broader interconnectedness of the human experience, affecting the collective moral consciousness and integrity of society as a whole.

Idolatry – Overview, Prohibition and Prevention:

Idolatry, a practice deeply ingrained in the history of humanity, has been addressed with utmost severity in the Quran. To fully comprehend the Quranic perspective on idolatry, it is essential to delve into its historical and theological roots. The origins of idolatry can be traced back to the earliest civilizations, where people fashioned physical representations of deities to embody their spiritual beliefs. These idols served as focal points for religious rituals and acts of devotion, becoming instrumental in shaping societal norms and practices.

Over time, idolatry evolved into a pervasive phenomenon across diverse cultures, perpetuating a complex web of beliefs and customs. From ancient Mesopotamia to the Indus Valley civilization, the allure of idol worship remained ubiquitous, manifesting in various forms and with varying degrees of significance. The Quran, in its comprehensive elucidation of monotheism, unequivocally opposes the veneration of idols and condemns the associated fallacious ideologies.

Within the theological framework of Islam, idolatry fundamentally contradicts the essence of Tawhid, the indivisible oneness of Allah, and constitutes a violation of faith. The Quran articulates that true submission to the divine transcends any tangible representation and necessitates absolute reliance on the unseen Creator. Furthermore, the Quran presents a piercing critique of idolatry by addressing its limitations and irrationality, debunking the notion of intermediaries between humankind and God. This theological discourse not only elucidates the inherent falsehood of polytheistic beliefs but also situates the concept of idolatry within the wider narrative of human spiritual evolution.

Additionally, the Quran provides clear and unequivocal guidance regarding the prohibition and prevention of idolatry, emphasizing the exclusive worship of the One True God. It is emphasized that the very foundation of faith lies in adhering to the oneness and uniqueness of God, without associating any partners or intermediaries. Quranic verses such as 'And your God is one God. There is no deity [worthy of worship] except Him, the Entirely Merciful, the Especially Merciful' (Quran 2:163) reinforce the absolute rejection of idol worship. Additionally, the Quran holds that idolatry obscures spiritual truth, leading individuals away from the righteous path and into darkness.

The Quran prescribes various preventive measures against idolatry, advocating for the cultivation of knowledge and understanding to recognize the futility of idol worship. It encourages critical thinking and reflection on the signs of God's majesty in the universe, guiding believers to find solace and enlightenment in the contemplation of creation. Furthermore, the Quran promotes sincere devotion and regular prayers as a means to fortify one's commitment to monotheism and thereby safeguard against the allure of idolatry. Ritual purity and spiritual discipline are also highlighted as essential practices to cleanse the heart and mind from the temptations of idol worship.

The Quranic prescriptions against idolatry are not merely confined to individual reflections, but extend to the societal level as well. The Quran emphasizes the importance of fostering a community built upon virtues of justice, compassion, and righteousness as a shield against the prevalence of idolatry. Additionally, it advocates for the eradication of social and economic disparities, recognizing that inequality can breed idolatrous tendencies rooted in covetousness and arrogance. Moreover, the promotion of ethical conduct and accountability within the community is underscored as a means to counteract the spread of idolatrous practices.

The Connection Between Faithfulness and Monotheism:

Faithfulness in Islam is deeply intertwined with the belief in monotheism, the concept of worshiping and recognizing the oneness of God. The Quran emphasizes the inseparable relationship between faithfulness and the monotheistic principles upheld by Muslims. At its core, monotheism represents a commitment to acknowledging the unity of the divine and directing all acts of worship and obedience solely to the one true God. This singular devotion serves as the foundation for faithfulness, guiding individuals to uphold moral and ethical standards in every aspect of their lives.

Central to the connection between faithfulness and monotheism is the tenet of tawhid, which underscores the unity, uniqueness, and sovereignty of God in Islam. Tawhid encapsulates the fundamental belief that there is no deity worthy of worship except Allah, and this principle lies at the heart of Islamic faithfulness. By recognizing the oneness of God and submitting to His will, adherents strive to maintain unwavering loyalty and fidelity in their spiritual and earthly endeavors.

Moreover, monotheism in Islam extends beyond a theological concept; it permeates various facets of an individual's existence, fostering upright conduct, compassion, and justice. The unity of God not only informs the private devotions of believers but also shapes their interactions with others, emphasizing the importance of embodying virtuous behavior and treating fellow beings with dignity and fairness. This integral link between faithfulness and monotheism elucidates the ethical framework that guides Muslims in their quest for righteousness and benevolence.

Faithfulness rooted in monotheism engenders a sense of accountability and responsibility toward both the Creator and creation. It instills an understanding of the interconnectedness between belief in the oneness of God and the fulfillment of one's obligations and duties towards the wider community. As such, faithfulness becomes a lived expression of monotheism, manifesting in acts of charity, philanthropy, and social engagement, exemplifying the holistic nature of Islamic monotheistic principles.

Chapter XXVIII
FAITH AS A WAY OF LIFE

Islamic life principles are deeply rooted in the teachings of the Quran and the traditions of Prophet Muhammad. These principles form the foundation upon which a Muslim's daily life is built, guiding their thoughts, actions, and interactions with others. At the core of Islamic life principles is the concept of Tawhid, the belief in the oneness of Allah and His absolute sovereignty. This principle influences every aspect of a Muslim's life, shaping their worldview and ethical framework. Additionally, the practice of Salah (prayer) serves as a constant reminder of one's purpose and connection to the divine. The five daily prayers not only provide spiritual nourishment but also serve as a means of seeking guidance and assistance from Allah in facing life's challenges. Zakat, the giving of alms to those in need, underscores the importance of charity and compassion, fostering a sense of community and solidarity among Muslims. The observance of Ramadan, with its emphasis on self-discipline, self-reflection, and empathy for the less fortunate, reinforces the value of humility and empathy. The performance of Hajj, the pilgrimage to the holy city of Mecca, highlights the unity of the global Muslim community and the significance of collective worship. Islamic life principles also emphasize the importance of upholding justice, kindness, and honesty in all dealings, whether personal, professional, or social. Furthermore, the practice of continuous learning and reflection through the pursuit of knowledge is encouraged, nurturing intellectual growth and moral development. By embracing these foundational principles, Muslims strive to lead a life that is in harmony with the divine will and conducive to personal and communal well-being. As such, the integration of these principles into daily life fosters a deep sense of purpose, meaning, and spiritual fulfillment for individuals, while also contributing to the enrichment and cohesion of society at large.

Daily Practices and Rituals - Foundations of Faith:

From the pre-dawn Fajr prayer to the final Isha prayer at night, the five daily prayers are a cornerstone of a Muslim's spiritual routine. These prayers punctuate the day, serving as constant reminders of one's connection to the divine. The ritual ablutions (wudu) performed before each prayer symbolize purification, both physical and spiritual, preparing the worshipper to stand before their Creator.

Beyond the obligatory prayers, additional acts of worship, such as the voluntary Sunnah prayers, supplications (duas), and remembrance of God (dhikr) further enrich the spiritual tapestry of a Muslim's life. The practice of fasting during the month of Ramadan cultivates self-discipline, empathy, and an acute awareness of the blessings bestowed by the Almighty. Similarly, the annual pilgrimage to Mecca, known as Hajj, underscores the unity of the Muslim community and the legacy of Prophet Ibrahim.

In addition to these acts of worship, adherence to the prophetic traditions (Sunnah) and following the guidance of the Quran shape the minutiae of daily life for a practicing Muslim. Modesty in attire, honesty in dealings, kindness to neighbors, and concern for the vulnerable are among the virtues instilled through these teachings. The integration of faith into everyday actions emphasizes the holistic nature of Islamic practice, transcending ritual obligations to encompass ethical conduct and social responsibility.

The call to prayer (adhan) echoing across cities and villages, inviting believers to leave the transient concerns of the world and turn to the eternal verities of faith, underscores the centrality of these daily practices. Through the repetition of these rituals, believers affirm their commitment to God and fortify their spiritual resilience amidst the ebb and flow of worldly affairs. Thus, the daily practices and rituals within Islam not only provide a framework for personal piety but also establish a shared rhythm that unites Muslims across diverse cultures and geographies.

The Role of Family and Community in Sustaining Faith:

The familial structure, with its emphasis on love, care, and mutual support, serves as a nurturing environment for the practice and preservation of religious beliefs. Within the family, individuals learn essential values, ethics, and rituals that form the bedrock of their faith. Parents play a crucial role as they impart the teachings of Islam to their children, instilling within them a sense of identity and purpose rooted in their religious heritage.

Furthermore, the broader community also plays a pivotal role in sustaining faith. Mosques, madrasas, and community centers serve as hubs for spiritual development, education, and communal worship. These spaces provide opportunities for believers to come together, fostering a sense of unity, solidarity, and brotherhood. Through congregational prayers, religious gatherings, and social events, the community reinforces the shared values and principles of Islam, creating a support network that bolsters individual faith.

The intergenerational transmission of faith within families and the communal reinforcement of religious practices are integral to the holistic sustainability of faith. In times of joy and sorrow, the presence of a strong familial and communal support system can offer comfort, guidance, and a sense of belonging, strengthening one's resolve to adhere to the teachings of Islam.

Moreover, within the family and community settings, the concept of 'amr bil ma'ruf wa nahy anil munkar'—enjoining what is right and forbidding what is wrong—is upheld. This principle encourages individuals to promote virtue and discourage vice within their spheres of influence, thereby cultivating a culture of moral uprightness and mutual accountability.

The collaborative effort of families and communities in nurturing and sustaining faith serves to empower individuals, especially the younger generation, to uphold Islamic principles and values amidst the challenges of modernity. By fostering a sense of belonging and interconnectedness, the family and community unite believers in a shared commitment to living according to the tenets of Islam, thereby fortifying their faith and contributing to the vibrancy of the Muslim ummah.

Striving for Righteousness - Ethical and Moral Conduct:

In Islam, the concept of righteous conduct is deeply rooted in the teachings of the Quran and the example set by Prophet Muhammad. Ethical and moral conduct encompasses every facet of a Muslim's life, guiding their interactions with others, their decision-making processes, and their overall behavior. Central to this concept is the adherence to the principles of justice, compassion, honesty, and integrity in all dealings.

One of the fundamental ethical principles in Islam is the concept of 'Adl', or justice, which emphasizes fair treatment and equality for all individuals regardless of their backgrounds or beliefs. Upholding justice not only involves ensuring that one's actions are equitable and fair but also standing up for the rights of those who may be marginalized or oppressed. Muslims are encouraged to embody the values of empathy and compassion, demonstrating kindness and understanding towards others as exemplified by the Prophet's own conduct.

Furthermore, honesty and integrity constitute integral components of moral conduct in Islam. Muslims are advised to be truthful and sincere in their words and actions, striving to uphold the value of trustworthiness in their personal and professional lives. The Quran commands believers to 'speak the truth even if it is against yourselves' (Quran 4:135), emphasizing the importance of transparency and sincerity in all communications and transactions.

An essential aspect of ethical conduct is the fulfillment of responsibilities towards oneself, family, and community. The Quran and Sunnah emphasize the significance of maintaining strong familial ties, fulfilling financial obligations, and actively participating in charitable endeavors as means of contributing to the welfare of society at large. Additionally, the concept of 'Amanah', or trust, underscores the responsibility Muslims have in honoring commitments and safeguarding entrusted possessions or information of others.

Moreover, Islam places great emphasis on self-discipline and self-restraint, promoting moderation and balance in all aspects of life. This includes managing one's desires and inclinations, demonstrating patience in adversity, and displaying gratitude during times of success and prosperity. By cultivating these virtues, individuals strive to attain righteousness and moral uprightness, aligning their conduct with the values prescribed in Islamic teachings.

Facing Trials with Patience and Gratitude:

Trials and tribulations are an inevitable part of human existence, and the Islamic perspective offers insights on how to front on to them with resilience. Central to this approach is the concept of sabr, or patience, which involves hardships with steadfastness and fortitude. The Quran teaches that adversity is a test from Allah, and the way one responds to these trials has spiritual implications. Instead of succumbing to despair or anguish, Muslims are encouraged to exhibit sabr as a means of drawing closer to their Creator.

In addition to patience, gratitude is another key virtue emphasized in Islamic teachings when confronting trials. Expressing gratitude during times of difficulty may seem counterintuitive, but it is a powerful means of finding solace and maintaining a positive outlook. By acknowledging blessings amidst challenges, individuals can cultivate a sense of contentment and humility, recognizing that even in moments of strife, there is much for which to be grateful.

The Prophet Muhammad (peace be upon him) serves as an exemplar in demonstrating patience and gratitude in the face of adversity. His unwavering composure during periods of hardship and persecution provides a model for Muslims seeking guidance in facing their own trials. Through his example, believers are inspired to persevere with patience and express gratitude, regardless of the circumstances they encounter.

Moreover, Islamic tradition offers practical tools for developing patience and gratitude in the face of trials. Regular remembrance of Allah through dhikr, prayer, and seeking closeness to God through acts of worship are integral components in building resilience and maintaining faith during challenging times. Additionally, engaging in charitable acts and helping those in need can serve as meaningful reminders of the blessings bestowed upon an individual, fostering a spirit of gratitude and compassion.

Preparation for the Journey Beyond - Death in Islam:

In Islamic teachings, the concept of death is deeply intertwined with the nature of life itself. Muslims are encouraged to contemplate and prepare for the inevitable journey beyond this temporal existence, viewing death not as an end but as a transition to the everlasting Hereafter. This mindset influences the actions, attitudes, and beliefs of individuals within the Islamic faith. Preparation for the journey beyond in Islam encompasses spiritual, emotional, and practical aspects.

Spiritually, Muslims are taught to live their lives in constant awareness of the ephemeral nature of worldly existence, enjoining righteousness, kindness, and humility. The Quran and Hadith provide guidance on how to lead a virtuous life, emphasizing the need to continually seek repentance, perform good deeds, and uphold the principles of justice and compassion. Such spiritual preparedness is considered essential for a smooth transition into the next realm.

Emotionally, Islam encourages believers to confront the reality of mortality with patience, serenity, and trust in the divine wisdom and mercy. The concept of qadr, or predestination, plays a crucial role in shaping the Muslim attitude towards death, offering solace and reassurance in times of bereavement. Through prayers, remembrance of God, and support from the community, individuals are taught to find strength and comfort as they face the inevitability of their own eventual departure.

Practically, Islam provides specific guidelines for handling various aspects related to death, including the rituals of washing and shrouding the deceased, conducting the funeral prayer, and burying the deceased in accordance with Islamic traditions. Additionally, estate planning, distribution of inheritance, and fulfilling any outstanding obligations towards family and society are considered integral parts of preparing for the journey beyond. These practical preparations help ensure a dignified and respectful transition for the departed and ease the burden on those left behind.

The topic of death and the preparation for the journey beyond in Islam serve as constant reminders for Muslims to lead purposeful lives, prioritize meaningful relationships, and strive for continuous self-improvement. By internalizing the teachings related to death, adherents of the faith seek to live with greater mindfulness, compassion, and gratitude, recognizing that their actions in this world have lasting implications in the realm of eternity.

Legacy and Remembrance - Leaving a Mark of Faith:

In Islam, the concept of legacy goes beyond material possessions and worldly achievements. It encompasses the lasting impact a person leaves on the world, particularly in terms of their faith, character, and contributions to society. The idea of leaving a mark of faith is deeply rooted in the teachings of Islam and reflects the emphasis on the eternal nature of the soul and the accountability individuals will face in the Hereafter.

One of the primary ways in which Muslims seek to leave a lasting legacy of faith is through acts of charity, philanthropy, and community service. These actions not only benefit those in need but also serve as a form of ongoing charity (sadaqah jariyah) that continues to accrue rewards for the individual even after their passing. Whether it's building a well to provide clean water, funding educational initiatives, or supporting humanitarian causes, these endeavors symbolize a commitment to improving the welfare of others and reflect the individual's dedication to fulfilling their moral and religious obligations.

Moreover, the establishment of endowments (waqf) plays a crucial role in ensuring the perpetuation of beneficial services for the community. From mosques and schools to hospitals and libraries, endowments have historically served as institutions that contribute to the spiritual, educational, and social development of society. By contributing to or initiating such efforts, individuals aim to leave behind a tangible legacy that continues to benefit future generations and earns them continuous rewards in the sight of God.

Beyond material contributions, the impact of one's character and conduct on succeeding generations holds immense significance in Islamic tradition. Upholding moral integrity, displaying kindness and compassion, and embodying the teachings of the Quran and the Prophet Muhammad (peace be upon him) are fundamental to leaving a positive impression that inspires others to follow the same path. This involves being an exemplar of honesty, justice, and humility, as well as nurturing strong family ties, fostering unity within the community, and engaging in dawah (inviting to the faith) with wisdom and beautiful preaching. In doing so, individuals not only leave a personal legacy of righteousness but also contribute to the preservation and propagation of Islamic values.

Finally, the aspect of remembrance and supplication for the deceased is integral to leaving a mark of faith. Engaging in continuous prayer, recitation of the Quran, and acts of charity on behalf of loved ones who have passed away demonstrates a commitment to honoring their memory and seeking God's mercy and forgiveness for them. This practice also serves as a means of inspiring others to recognize the value of cherishing the heritage and virtues of those who have departed, reinforcing the belief in the continued relevance of their influence on present and future generations.

As Muslims strive to leave a mark of faith, they are reminded of the transient nature of worldly life and the perpetual nature of the hereafter. By focusing on building a legacy rooted in faith, righteousness, and service to humanity, individuals endeavor to create a meaningful impact that transcends their earthly existence and resonates in the divine realm.

The Interplay of Faith and Practice:

In Islam, the interplay of faith and practice is emphasized as an integrated approach to living a holistic and morally upright life. Faith in Islam is not merely a set of beliefs confined to theological concepts; rather, it is intertwined with practical aspects of daily living. This integrated approach is designed to guide Muslims in harmonizing their beliefs with their actions, thereby creating a cohesive and spiritually fulfilling existence.

The Quran and the teachings of Prophet Muhammad (peace be upon him) provide comprehensive guidance on how to integrate faith into every aspect of life. From personal conduct to social interactions, the principles of Islamic faith are meant to permeate all spheres of human existence, fostering an environment of compassion, justice, and righteousness. At the core of this integrated approach is the acknowledgment that one's faith should manifest in one's behavior and treatment of others. It emphasizes the importance of being honest, compassionate, and generous, thereby fostering a society built on mutual respect and consideration.

Additionally, the integrated approach of faith and practice urges individuals to demonstrate humility, patience, and sincerity in their endeavors. By embodying these qualities, Muslims aim to emulate the noble character of Prophet Muhammad and adhere to the ethical framework outlined in the Quran. Furthermore, this integrated approach extends to matters of community engagement and societal welfare.

Muslims are encouraged to actively participate in charitable activities, promote social justice, and contribute to the betterment of their communities. This proactive involvement serves as a reflection of their faith in action, demonstrating their commitment to uplifting humanity and fostering a more just and equitable society.

Ultimately, the integrated approach of faith and practice in Islam is underpinned by the notion that true belief necessitates conscientious action. It inspires individuals to lead purposeful lives, rooted in spiritual devotion and moral uprightness, while actively contributing to the well-being of society. By integrating their faith into their everyday actions, Muslims strive to exemplify the values of compassion, integrity, and benevolence, thereby actualizing the impact of faith on their lives and the world around them.

Chapter XXIX
DEATH

Death in the Quran:

Death holds a significance in Islamic teachings, as the Quran offers divine insights and wisdom on this inevitable reality. The Quran emphasizes the transient nature of earthly life, urging believers to contemplate the brevity of existence and the certainty of mortality. Through various verses, the Quran provides deep reflections on the purpose of life and the inevitability of death, guiding individuals to seek spiritual enlightenment and prepare for the Hereafter.

The Quran elucidates that every soul will taste death, underscoring the universal and inescapable nature of this journey from earthly life to the afterlife. This recognition instills a sense of humility and contemplation, prompting individuals to reevaluate their priorities and actions in light of the broader spiritual context. By acknowledging death as a fundamental aspect of human existence, the Quran encourages believers to strive for righteous deeds, seeking to attain harmony with divine virtues and values.

Furthermore, the Quran imparts wisdom regarding the transient nature of worldly possessions and achievements, emphasizing the ephemeral nature of material wealth and status in the face of mortality. This perspective fosters a detachment from materialism and a deeper focus on eternal values, encouraging individuals to invest in virtuous conduct and beneficial contributions that extend beyond the constraints of temporal life.

In addressing death, the Quran also illuminates the interconnectedness of life and the continuity of existence beyond the physical realm. Quranic teachings convey the concept of a soul's progression into the Hereafter, underscoring the nature of spiritual identity and accountability beyond mortal life. This insight offers solace and perspective, guiding believers to approach death with steadfastness and assurance in the boundless mercy and justice of the Divine.

Reflections on Mortality:

Mortality and the limited duration of human existence are central themes in Islamic theology and spirituality, shaping the way Muslims perceive life and prepare for the afterlife. In Islamic tradition, reflections on mortality serve as a reminder of the fleeting nature of this worldly life, prompting believers to engage in righteous deeds and mindfulness of their moral responsibilities. The Quran offers insights into the impermanence of life, emphasizing that every soul will taste death and encouraging believers to contemplate the transient nature of existence.

From an Islamic perspective, acknowledging mortality fosters a deep sense of humility and gratitude, reminding individuals of their dependence on the divine will and the necessity of living with moral consciousness. Furthermore, the awareness of mortality underscores the essential value of time, compelling Muslims to prioritize actions that align with their spiritual values and contribute positively to the world.

Consequently, the Islamic viewpoint on mortality extends beyond the individual, encompassing the broader societal and ethical implications of impermanence. Understanding that life is finite encourages Muslims to build meaningful relationships, resolve conflicts, seek justice, and strive for social harmony. Such reflections on mortality cultivate a holistic approach to life, where personal growth and community welfare are interconnected facets of a fulfilling existence.

In practical terms, the Islamic perspective on mortality promotes the establishment of legacies through acts of charity, compassion, and benevolence. This serves as a testament to the belief in the eternal impact of virtuous deeds, transcending individual lifespans and resonating across generations. Moreover, contemplating mortality instills a sense of accountability, prompting individuals to live authentically, uphold ethical principles, and seek continuous self-improvement.

Preparatory Practices for the Afterlife:

In Islam, the concept of death is deeply intertwined with the idea of the afterlife. It is believed that death is merely a transition from the temporary worldly life to an eternal existence in the hereafter. As such, Islam provides a comprehensive framework for preparing for the afterlife through various practical and spiritual practices. One essential preparatory practice is engaging in acts of worship and devotion, such as performing the five daily prayers, giving charity, and fasting during Ramadan. These acts not only strengthen one's connection with Allah but also serve as a means of seeking forgiveness and earning reward for the eternal life to come.

Moreover, the concept of Sadaqah Jariyah, or continuous charity, holds immense significance in Islamic teachings. Engaging in charitable acts that have a lasting positive impact, such as building a mosque, digging a well, or supporting educational initiatives, is believed to bring ongoing rewards even after one's earthly life has ended, thereby enhancing their standing in the afterlife.

Self-reflection and self-improvement are also integral aspects of preparing for the afterlife. Muslims are encouraged to engage in sincere introspection, recognize their shortcomings, seek repentance, and strive for personal growth in adherence to Islamic principles. This includes cultivating good character, practicing patience, showing kindness to others, and avoiding behaviors that are contrary to Islamic ethics.

Another vital preparatory practice is upholding family ties and fulfilling responsibilities towards one's relatives. In Islam, maintaining strong familial bonds and fulfilling obligations towards parents, spouses, children, and other family members hold immense importance. Acts such as providing for one's family, showing compassion towards parents, and fostering harmony within the family unit are viewed as means of earning divine favor and blessings in the afterlife.

Lastly, the remembrance of death and the remembrance of Allah play a crucial role in preparing for the afterlife. Constantly reflecting on the transient nature of earthly life and the certainty of death serves as a reminder to prioritize actions that bring spiritual benefit and align with the teachings of Islam. Additionally, engaging in the regular recitation of Quranic verses, supplications, and seeking forgiveness through Dhikr (remembrance) are considered effective means of purifying the soul and preparing for the eventual meeting with the Divine.

The Role of Faith in Facing Death:

In Islam, faith plays a central and transformative role in shaping one's approach to death and the afterlife. The concept of faith encompasses a deep-seated belief in the oneness and mercy of Allah, as well as a trust in the divine wisdom that governs all aspects of existence, including life's end.

At the core of Islamic teachings is the assurance that the soul continues its journey beyond physical death, further underscoring the pivotal influence of faith in shaping an individual's perception of transition. Believers are encouraged to embody unwavering faith in the knowledge that their earthly existence is but one phase of their eternal spiritual trajectory. Such conviction serves to instill a sense of purpose, serenity, and acceptance in the face of mortality, offering solace amidst the inherent uncertainties of life.

Moreover, faith provides a framework through which individuals can derive moral steadfastness and an understanding of the transient nature of worldly affairs. By cultivating a deep sense of spirituality and piety, adherents find themselves better equipped to confront the prospect of death with composure, humility, and gratitude for the gift of life bestowed upon them. Through devotion to prayer, reflection on Quranic guidance, and adherence to ethical principles, faith becomes an anchor that assists in facing mortal existence and contemplating the transcendental verities that underpin human destiny.

Furthermore, faith imbues individuals with the fortitude to confront the vicissitudes and trials of life with equanimity, knowing that each challenge encountered serves as an opportunity for spiritual growth and a means to attain closeness to the Divine. As such, the role of faith extends beyond providing solace in the face of mortality; it enables believers to embrace the inevitability of death as an integral component of their cosmic journey and as a catalyst for virtuous conduct and self-refinement.

In essence, the unwavering faith espoused in Islam acts as a source of strength, resilience, and tranquility when confronted with the reality of mortality. Grounded in the tenets of compassion, submission, and divine decree, faith empowers individuals to view the culmination of earthly life not as a conclusion, but as a spiritual transition towards the boundless mercy and grace promised by the Almighty. It serves as a lens through which the ephemeral nature of existence is juxtaposed against the eternal promise of divine recompense, fostering a sense of purpose, optimism, and hope throughout the cyclical journey of life, death, and transcendence.

Seeking Forgiveness and Reconciliation:

Seeking forgiveness and reconciliation form essential components of spiritual and emotional preparation for the inevitable transition from worldly life to eternal life in Islamic teachings. The process of seeking forgiveness involves acknowledging one's shortcomings, repenting sincerely, and striving to rectify any wrongdoings. It is an act of humility and accountability, reflecting an individual's understanding of their inherent fallibility and their commitment to self-improvement.

In Islam, seeking forgiveness is not merely a verbal request but a deeply introspective and transformative practice that encompasses genuine remorse and a resolve to embrace positive change. Furthermore, seeking reconciliation with others is a crucial aspect of spiritual readiness for the afterlife. It requires individuals to address any conflicts, grievances, or misunderstandings with sincerity and compassion, aiming to mend relationships and foster harmony within their social and communal spheres. This process underscores the importance of empathy, understanding, and the willingness to bridge the gaps that may have strained interpersonal connections.

The Quran emphasizes the significance of seeking forgiveness and reconciliation, portraying them as virtuous acts that lead to personal growth and spiritual enrichment. It encourages believers to reflect on their actions, seek pardon from both the Divine and those whom they may have wronged, and actively participate in efforts to restore peace and goodwill. The process of seeking forgiveness and reconciliation can be cathartic, offering individuals the opportunity to unburden themselves of emotional weight and cultivate a sense of inner peace. It enables them to embark on their spiritual journey with a clear conscience, unencumbered by unresolved conflicts or lingering feelings of resentment.

By engaging in these transformative practices, individuals not only prepare themselves for the transition to eternal life but also contribute to enhancing the fabric of their communities and fostering a culture of empathy and understanding. Ultimately, seeking forgiveness and reconciliation embodies the core Islamic principles of compassion, mercy, and ethical consciousness, serving as pivotal steps in the spiritual preparation for the eventual transcendence from this world to the next.

The Transition - From Worldly Life to Eternal Life:

As we ponder the inevitability of death, we are compelled to consider what lies beyond this transient existence. In Islamic tradition, the transition from earthly life to the eternal realm is a pivotal moment with spiritual implications that reverberate throughout eternity. The Quran presents a tapestry of teachings regarding the soul's journey after death, emphasizing the accountability and recompense that await individuals based on their actions in the mortal realm. This prospect underscores the gravity of the transition and the imperative of leading a righteous and virtuous life. The belief in the resurrection and the Day of Judgment infuses the contemplation of death with a sense of responsibility and purpose, shaping the conduct of adherents as they experience their worldly sojourn. The understanding of this transition serves as a guiding light, illuminating the path towards moral rectitude and spiritual growth. As such, reflections on the transition from worldly life to eternal life permeate Islamic thought, imbuing it with a deeply introspective and reflective character.

Commemorating the Deceased:

Within Islamic tradition, the commemoration of the deceased is marked by specific rituals and observances. Following the death of a Muslim, it is customary for family and friends to gather for prayers and remembrance. Additionally, charitable acts, such as giving alms or donating to the poor, are often performed on behalf of the deceased as a way to bring blessings to their soul. The recitation of Quranic verses and prayers for the departed are also integral parts of Islamic commemorations, serving as a source of spiritual comfort for the grieving individuals.

Moreover, various cultures around the world have distinct customs for commemorating the deceased, often incorporating elements of music, dance, and communal feasting. In some traditions, anniversaries of a person's passing are commemorated with elaborate ceremonies, from lighting candles to laying flowers at gravesites, symbolizing the presence of the departed in the hearts of the living. These rituals not only provide an opportunity for mourning but also seek to celebrate the life and legacy of the departed individual, emphasizing the continuity of their impact on the community.

The significance of commemorating the deceased extends beyond mere remembrance; it serves as a means to reinforce bonds within families and communities, providing a space for collective grief and healing. These rituals offer a framework through which individuals can come together to share their memories, offer condolences, and find support during times of loss. By engaging in these practices, individuals reaffirm the interconnectedness of humanity, recognizing the universal experience of loss and the need for empathy and solidarity in the face of bereavement.

Chapter XXX
LIFE AFTER DEATH

As stated in the Quran, in the center of the afterlife belief system is the concept of accountability and recompense in the hereafter. The afterlife in Islam is not merely a distant realm but a significant dimension that permeates the entirety of earthly existence and underpins the ethical and metaphysical outlook of adherents. It offers a compelling lens through which to contemplate the transient nature of worldly life and the consequences of one's actions beyond the confines of mortality. Moreover, the teachings regarding the afterlife foster a sense of purpose, responsibility, and ultimate justice, reinforcing the notion that life is a continuum that extends beyond the present temporal domain. This robust theological framework provides an impetus for ethical conduct, mindfulness, and spiritual fortitude, offering solace and assurance to believers amidst the trials and tribulations of life. Embracing the multifaceted notions of paradise, hell, resurrection, and divine mercy, the Islamic perspective on the afterlife proffers a holistic paradigm that weaves together the individual, societal, and cosmic dimensions of human existence. Understanding and internalizing these foundational beliefs engenders a deep sense of humility, gratitude, and vigilance, fostering a steadfast commitment to righteousness and compassion.

Barzakh -The Intermediate Realm

In Islamic eschatology, the concept of Barzakh represents the intermediate realm between death and the Day of Judgment. Derived from Arabic roots meaning 'barrier' or 'isthmus,' Barzakh serves as a transitional state for the souls of the deceased. This period is believed to be spiritually meaningful, as it marks the separation of the soul from the body while awaiting the final judgment by Allah.

According to Islamic teachings, the state of Barzakh is not constrained by time or space as experienced in the earthly life. Rather, it is a dimension where the departed souls undergo a period of reflection and accountability for their actions in the mortal world. While the physical body disintegrates, the soul enters a phase of introspection and contemplation, which shapes its subsequent destiny in the afterlife.

The Quran elucidates the concept of Barzakh through allegorical and symbolic descriptions, emphasizing the nature of this intermediate realm. It emphasizes that the experiences during Barzakh are distinct from those in the earthly life, distinct yet connected to the soul's ultimate fate. Within this realm, the departed undergo both solace and torment based on their deeds, setting the stage for their reckoning on the Day of Judgment.

Islamic scholars and theologians have delved deeply into interpreting the nature of Barzakh, exploring its metaphysical dimensions and implications for human existence. Their scholarship has shed light on the transformative potential inherent in this interim period, highlighting the importance of leading a virtuous and righteous life. Through understanding the concept of Barzakh, Muslims are motivated to uphold moral integrity and spiritual consciousness, recognizing that their actions carry repercussions even beyond the confines of worldly existence.

Moreover, reflections on Barzakh serve to deepen believers' awareness of the interconnectedness of the material and spiritual realms. This intermediate state underscores the continuance of the human soul and its journey toward divine justice and mercy. Understanding Barzakh fosters a sense of accountability and purpose, urging individuals to conduct themselves with mindfulness and conscientiousness in every facet of their lives.

Day of Judgment:

The Day of Judgment serves as an essential tenet that underscores the eventual accountability and recompense for every individual's deeds. This pivotal event is deeply rooted in the belief that all human beings, from the dawn of existence until the end of time, will stand before the Almighty to answer for their actions on Earth. The Quran elucidates this momentous occasion with vivid imagery, portraying a scene of unparalleled solemnity and gravity, where all creations will be brought forth and summoned to stand before the Divine Court of Justice. It is a day when no soul can intercede on behalf of another, and each person will face the unerring justice of God. The revelation provides a comprehensive account of the events leading up to the Day of Judgment, detailing the signs that will manifest as the world inches closer to its ultimate culmination. The prophetic traditions expound further on the severity and intensity of the reckoning, underscoring the magnitude of the impending judgment. The subjects of resurrection, gathering, and the unfolding of individual records are elucidated in great detail, instilling a sense of urgency and mindfulness in the minds of believers. The descriptions of this apocalyptic scenario serve as a powerful motivator for adherents to lead a life of righteousness and conscientiousness, emphasizing the inevitability of being held accountable for their actions. The doctrine of the Day of Judgment not only serves as a moral compass for adherents but also offers solace and hope, assuring those who have faced adversity and persecution in the temporal realm that justice will ultimately prevail. It embodies the pinnacle of divine wisdom and exemplifies the absolute fairness and impartiality of God's judgment, reaffirming the ethos of equitability and uprightness in Islam.

Paradise:

Paradise, or Jannah in Arabic, is described as a garden adorned with lush greenery, flowing rivers, and fruits of all kinds, promising an abundance of provisions for its inhabitants. The imagery of heavenly gardens, fragrant blooms, and refreshing streams portrays an idyllic environment that transcends earthly pleasures. Moreover, the Quran paints a picture of Jannah as a realm where inhabitants will experience spiritual contentment, joy, and peace beyond imagination. Furthermore, the concept of companionship in Jannah is highlighted, emphasizing the reunion with loved ones and the pleasure of communal gatherings. The attire, dwellings, and luxuries of Jannah are depicted as exquisite beyond measure, symbolizing the ultimate reward for a life lived in obedience to God's commandments. The Quran also elucidates that the rewards in Jannah are not merely material but extend to the eternal proximity to the divine presence. The believers will bask in the pleasure of beholding Allah and experiencing His boundless mercy and love. This vision serves as a source of hope and motivation, guiding individuals to strive for righteousness and attain the pinnacle of spiritual success. Moreover, the description of Jannah encompasses the concept of everlasting happiness and fulfillment, free from suffering, pain, and sorrow. It conveys the idea of a state of eternal bliss, where the blessings and delights never fade, providing a contrast to the transitory nature of worldly pleasures.

Hell:

Hell, or Jahannam, in Islamic belief constitutes a realm of unimaginable suffering and torment, destined for those who repeatedly transgress the boundaries of moral conduct. Descriptions of this abode are plentiful within Islamic scripture and tradition, providing vivid imagery of the consequences awaiting those who deviate from the path of righteousness. The Quran depicts Hell as a place of intense heat and scorching winds, with its inhabitants excruciating punishment for their deeds on earth.

The severity of punishments in Hell is portrayed as just recompense for the types of sins committed during one's earthly life. The Quran illustrates the agonizing ordeal that awaits wrongdoers, emphasizing that they will be subjected to the torment of fire and boiling water, creating an unrelenting sense of despair and remorse. It is through these descriptions that believers are reminded of the consequences of their actions and guided towards upholding ethical and virtuous behavior.

Moreover, Islamic teachings emphasize that Hell is not merely a physical realm of punishment, but also a spiritual state reflecting the anguish and regret experienced by its denizens. The moral significance of these depictions lies in their ability to instill an awareness of accountability and conscience among adherents, prompting them to reflect on their choices and strive for spiritual purification.

The depiction of Hell in Islamic thought serves as a solemn reminder of the consequences of straying from the path of righteousness and virtue. It underscores the significance of leading a life guided by ethical principles and mindfulness, and emphasizes the potential repercussions of succumbing to base desires and immoral conduct. Central to the teachings is the idea that individuals possess free will and agency, yet must also bear the responsibility for the consequences arising from their decisions and actions.

Furthermore, the concept of redemption and mercy remains integral within Islamic discourse, offering believers the opportunity to seek repentance and forgiveness, thereby transcending the implications of their previous misdeeds. This duality between accountability and clemency thus forms a recurring theme within discussions of Hell, balancing the weight of consequences with the prospect of spiritual renewal and reformation.

The Role of Angels in the Afterlife:

In Islamic belief, angels play a significant role in the afterlife, serving as intermediaries between Allah and humanity. These celestial beings are viewed as pure and obedient entities created by Allah to carry out various tasks, including those related to the transition from earthly life to the afterlife. According to Islamic teachings, angels are responsible for a person's record-keeping of deeds during their lifetime. They meticulously document every action, word, and even intention of individuals, which will be used as evidence on the Day of Judgment. The Archangel Israfil is assigned the crucial task of blowing the trumpet to signal the apocalypse and the commencement of the Day of Judgment. In this context, angels act as divine instruments for the execution of justice and accountability in the afterlife.

Moreover, angels feature prominently in the process of guiding souls to their final abodes. It is believed that upon death, two angels, Munkar and Nakir, visit the deceased in their graves to question them about their faith and deeds. Subsequently, they assist in the soul's journey toward the realm of Barzakh, where it undergoes a period of examination before the ultimate resurrection. Furthermore, angels participate in the allocation of rewards and punishments, ensuring that divine justice is carried out equitably to reflect an individual's earthly actions.

In addition to their role as custodians of divine justice, angels are also associated with the presentation of the delights of

Paradise and the torments of Hell to the souls awaiting judgment. This portrayal emphasizes the impactful roles angels hold in shaping the perceptions of the afterlife for individuals. Their presence serves as a reminder of the implications of one's choices and behaviors and reinforces the concept of accountability in the Hereafter.

Moreover, angels are integral to the concept of spiritual protection and guidance while individuals are living. Muslims believe that each person has angelic guardians who record their good and bad deeds and intercede on their behalf when they repent sincerely. Hence, the presence and involvement of angels in both earthly life and the afterlife exemplify their essential role in the Islamic worldview, thereby influencing human conduct and consciousness.

Soul's Journey - From Death to Final Abode:

As the physical body ceases to function, the soul embarks on a journey from the realm of the living to its final destination. Islam delineates a detailed account of this transition, enveloped in spiritual significance. Upon separation from the corporeal vessel, the soul is met by angels who guide it through a series of stages, each bearing immense weight in determining its ultimate abode. This journey is marked by awe-inspiring events and reckonings, where the soul witnesses the consequences of its earthly actions. According to Islamic teachings, the righteous are greeted by comforting experiences, while the wrongdoers face tribulations and remorse.

Bound by divine decree, the soul traverses through realms beyond human perception, encountering celestial wonders and undergoing evaluations that mirror the ethical fabric of its terrestrial existence. Throughout this journey, the soul remains tethered to its deeds and disposition during worldly life, as they shape its passage towards either spiritual ascent or descent. The Quran vividly illustrates these stages, offering believers a glimpse into this awe-inspiring odyssey, serving as both a source of comfort and admonishment.

Notably, the journey culminates in the reckoning before the Almighty, a juncture wherein every soul stands bared before the essence of truth. Here, the tapestry of one's existence unfolds, unraveling faith, conduct, and intentions. Every deed, word, and thought are laid bare, prompting a sense of accountability that transcends earthly perceptions. Such a reckoning instills a deep sense of awe in the soul, shaping its destiny in the afterlife.

Furthermore, Islamic tradition emphasizes the significance of prayers, charitable acts, and virtuous conduct during earthly life, as they serve as provisions for the soul's journey beyond this world. The notion of a graceful transition to the afterlife underscores the importance of leading a righteous and conscientious life, premised on divine guidance and moral rectitude. This understanding fundamentally shapes the outlook and conduct of believers, permeating their lives with steadfastness, benevolence, and an unwavering commitment to spiritual elevation.

Chapter XXXI
50 KEY QUOTES FROM THE PROPHET MUHAMMAD

1.
"The strong person is the one who can control himself when he is angry"

2.
"The seeking of knowledge is obligatory for every Muslim."

3.
"The best of houses is the house where an orphan gets love and kindness."

4.
"A good man treats women with honour."

5.
"God does not look at your forms and possessions but he looks at your hearts and your deeds."

6.
"The greatest of richness is the richness of the soul."

7.
"The strongest among you is the one who controls his anger."

8.
"Tell people of glad tidings and do not push them away."

9.
"He is not a true believer who eats his fill while his neighbour is hungry."

10.

"Seek knowledge from cradle to the grave."

11.
"A father gives nothing better than good education."

12.
"The elderly are the sources of mercy and divine blessing."

13.
"The best among you is the one who doesn't harm others with his tongue and hands."

14.
"The best among you are those who have the best manners and character."

15.
"Be kind, for whenever kindness becomes part of something, it beautifies it."

16.
"Riches are not from an abundance of worldly good but from a contented mind."

17.
"No two things have been combined better than knowledge and patience."

18.
"When a thing disturbs the peace of your heart, give it up."

19.
"There is reward for kindness to every living thing."

20.
"Strive always to excel in virtue and truth."

21.
"What has reached you was never meant to miss you, and what has missed you was never meant to reach you."

22.
"A kind word is a form of charity."

23.
"However much the faith of a man increases, his regard for women increases."

24.
"The worldly comforts are not for me."

25.
"Speak good or remain silent."

26.
"The believer does not slander, curse, or speak in an obscene or foul manner."

27.
"Lying would negatively influence your livelihood."

28.
"Feed the hungry and visit a sick person, and free the captive, if he be unjustly confined."

29.
"Assist any person oppressed whether Muslim or non-Muslim."

30.
"Do not waste water even if you were at a running stream."

31.
"A white has no superiority over a black nor a black has any superiority over white except by piety and good actions."

32.
"Look to those, who have been given less."

33.
"The greatest jihad is to battle your own soul, to fight the evil within yourself."

34.
"Exchange gifts, you will love one another."

35.
"Remember your own faults when you want to mention of others."

36.
"Those who are patient in adversity and forgive wrongs are the doers of excellence."

37.
"There are two blessings to which no one gives thanks: security and health."

38.
"It is one of the greatest sins that a man should curse his parents."

39.
"Those who are the means of good deeds are the same as those who perform good deeds."

40.
"Wisdom and knowledge are things that the believer lacks."

41.
"Those people who show no mercy will receive no mercy from Allah."

42.
"What is learned during youth, like an engraving on a stone, will never be forgotten."

43.
"Heaven lies beneath the feet of mothers."

44.
"Respecting a Muslim elderly is like showing respect to Allah."

45.
"The one who gets married has completed half of his/her religion."

46.
"The kindest, most amiable, generous, patient, and just among you is the closest to me in manner."

47.
"Be childlike with children."

48.
"Being like your father is one of the best blessings of Allah to you."

49.
"When Allah wants to pour His blessings upon you, He endows you with a Good Friend."

50.
"Causing harm to yourself and others is forbidden in Islam."